Gender
in Early
Childhood
Education

Gender
in Early
Childhood
Education

Implementing a Gender
Flexible Pedagogy

JO WARIN

Los Angeles | London | New Delhi
Singapore | Washington DC | Melbourne

Los Angeles | London | New Delhi
Singapore | Washington DC | Melbourne

SAGE Publications Ltd
1 Oliver's Yard
55 City Road
London EC1Y 1SP

SAGE Publications Inc.
2455 Teller Road
Thousand Oaks, California 91320

SAGE Publications India Pvt Ltd
B 1/I 1 Mohan Cooperative Industrial Area
Mathura Road
New Delhi 110 044

SAGE Publications Asia-Pacific Pte Ltd
3 Church Street
#10-04 Samsung Hub
Singapore 049483

Library of Congress Control Number: 2022942322

British Library Cataloguing in Publication data

A catalogue record for this book is available from the British Library

Editor: Delayna Spencer
Editorial assistant: Bali Birch-Lee
Production editor: Victoria Nicholas
Marketing manager: Lorna Patkai
Cover design: Wendy Scott
Typeset by: TNQ Technologies
Printed in the UK

ISBN 978-1-5297-4325-8
ISBN 978-1-5297-4324-1 (pbk)

At SAGE we take sustainability seriously. Most of our products are printed in the UK using responsibly sourced papers and boards. When we print overseas we ensure sustainable papers are used as measured by the PREPS grading system. We undertake an annual audit to monitor our sustainability.

For a new generation who will welcome in a spirit of gender flexibility, playfulness and creativity.

Contents

About the Author

Jo Warin is Professor in Gender and Social Relationships in Education at Lancaster University where she has been employed since 2001. She is director of the Doctoral Programme in Education and Social Justice and supervises many PhD students, with over 35 supervised to successful completion.

Through various published research articles, books and chapters, Jo has argued for and evidenced the concept of a gender flexible pedagogy: gender-sensitive teachers delivering a gender-sensitive curriculum. Her research draws on theories of masculinities and queer theory to analyse how gender is implicated in early childhood educational policy and practice. She has built an internationally recognised body of research about men's participation as teachers in early childhood education and care including her recent ESRC study into the recruitment and support of male early childhood educators – the GenderEYE project.

Jo also has a longstanding research trajectory in the social and emotional development of children and young people.

About This Book

The book is a stimulus and resource for all those who are interested in deconstructing the gender binary and who recognise the value of leading the way in early childhood education (ECE). It aims to promote the concept of a 'gender flexible pedagogy', an approach to the teaching and learning of young children that challenges gender stereotypes and the gender essentialist thinking that underpins them. The concept, originally introduced by Warin and Adriany (2017), is both practical and theoretical, based on teachers' modelling of gender flexible behaviour at the same time as providing resources and activities for children's own gender flexibility. This concept links together the three sections of the book which examine *what* a gender flexible approach means for curriculum, resources and activities in ECE, *who* can provide this approach and *how* it can be put into practice by a gender flexible workforce. These practical, replicable elements of the book are balanced with lively debate, scholarly discussion and questions for reader reflection. The book draws on the author's own extensive research in the field of gender and education for twenty years. This includes studies in Swedish and Norwegian ECE, case studies of male practitioners in English settings, an international collaborative study on men's career trajectories in the Early Years sector, and the recent GenderEYE project that explores support for the inclusion of more men in the Early Years sector. The book is a treasure trove of advice, examples of innovative classroom practice, thought-provoking case studies and clearly explained theories.

Keywords: early childhood education; gender flexible pedagogy; gender sensitivity; gender stereotypes; young children.

Acknowledgements

Lots of people have helped me write this book, generously giving their time, energy, moral support and expertise. I gratefully acknowledge their assistance.

I want to thank my readers of draft chapters, people who work 'at the chalk face' and who were able to put me right when I became too idealistic and unrealistic: Lizzie Cotton; Sam Quail; Hannah Quail. I hope that when you read this book you will see how you have influenced it. I am also very grateful to various experts I have consulted with and who have contributed to the case studies in this book, sometimes anonymously.

I am delighted with the onion illustration created by Anna Warin depicting the layers of gender theory I have presented here. Do check out her art on her Instagram page: aw_designs._

The research studies that I have led in recent times (*GenderEYE*; *Acorns*; *Swedish network in gender, teaching and care*) have been funded by the Economic and Social Research Council (ESRC), United Kingdom; Childbase Partnership; the Swedish Research Council. I gratefully acknowledge this funding. These studies have been carried out by excellent research teams. I count myself very fortunate to have had such committed and creative researchers to work with: Joann Wilkinson; Jeremy Davies; Helen Greaves; and Kari Emilsen (who all worked with me on the Gender-EYE project); Chris Marlow (who worked with me on the Acorns project); Annette Hellmann, Inga Wernersson; Eva Gannerud; Vina Adriany (who comprised the key team in our Swedish funded *Network in Gender, Teaching and Care*).

Special thanks to two inspirational PhD students who completed their theses many years ago and who have now gone on to productive careers in higher education/teacher education specialising in gender and who continue to influence my ideas. I have learned so much from them: Vina Adriany has opened up a critique of child-centredness which continues to influence my thinking; Jo Josepehidou has helped me to gain insights into the practicalities of undertaking gender-sensitive teacher training.

I also feel very lucky in my recent participation within a large international team, led by David Brody on *Men's Career Trajectories in ECEC* (see Brody et al., 2021) and I am grateful to Tim Rohrmann who convenes the *EECERA SIG in Gender Balance* that formed the context and launch pad for this wonderful collaborative project. I want to acknowledge the rich conversations we have had in this group with special thanks to David, Tim and Kari Emilsen as well as our other international partners.

Finally, and most importantly, on the home front, my thanks as always to my partner Pete for the loyal, reliable and steady forms of support he continues to provide.

1

Introduction: The Value of a Gender Flexible Pedagogy

Introduction

This book is intended as a resource for all those who are interested in dismantling the **gender binary** and who recognise the value of leading the way in the Early Years sector. It promotes the deconstruction of **gender stereotypes** with young children and offers a new concept for achieving this aim: the powerful and functional concept of a '**gender flexible pedagogy**'. This is based on teachers' modelling of gender flexible behaviour at the same time as the provision of resources and activities for children's own gender flexibility. It is written at a time of considerable public interest in matters concerned with gender and sexuality which has brought about a focus on the ways that educators can support positive changes in gender understandings and practices. The scope of the book is international and is based on an international research base, although a high proportion of the author's own research has been undertaken in the United Kingdom.

Aim of the Book: To Promote a Gender Flexible Pedagogy

The concept of a gender flexible pedagogy is practical, theoretically grounded and really useful to all those who have a professional or non-professional role in raising the next generation. It was introduced by Warin and Adriany (2017) to draw together two different foci of gender theory and practice in early childhood education. It combines ideas about the activities and resources that are deliberately made available to young children with ideas about teachers' behaviours and approaches. It interweaves staff modelling of alternative forms of masculinities and femininities together with explicit gender teaching within curricula. It has implications for both what is taught and how, for '**pedagogy**', incorporating implications for teachers and for teaching.

This concept can be turned into highly practical prescriptions for early childhood educators. These include ideas about how teachers can challenge gender stereotypes in their classrooms, the monitoring of resources for gender bias, how we can work with parents to reduce gender binary language, and how staff teams can collaborate to counter traditional gender roles in their own division of labour within the Early Years setting. So the key aim of this book is to promote this idea of a gender flexible pedagogy in early childhood education, and this concept will be a running theme throughout the book.

First, I want to contextualise this aim in two relevant and fairly recent societal changes:

- changes in perceptions and feelings about gender equality;
- an increasing value for children's 'voice', agency and well-being.

Sea Changes in Gender and Education

Gender

It feels as if we are currently on the crest of a large and forceful gender wave which has gathered momentum from the media, social media and everyday conversation, and is pushed along by more and more gender-focused research. Understandings of gender – how it is experienced and how it affects lives – are changing rapidly. For example the Everyday Sexism movement, commenced in 2012 by Laura Bates, has had a huge impact, creating an international resistance to a continuing toleration of abuse against women and girls. Relatedly, the social media #MeToo campaign became a tipping point for sexual harassment to be taken seriously. Tarana Burke originated the catchy 'Me Too' phrase in 2006 which was then popularised on a global scale in allegations directed at Harvey Weinstein and others to demonstrate the prevalence of sexual harassment and assault. These powerful international movements have led to the declaration that 'we are in the midst of a gender revolution' (*National Geographic*, January 2017). Gender equality is also prominent within the United Nation's Sustainable Development Goals (SDGs) (United Nations, 2021) where SDG number 5 aims to achieve gender equality and empower all women and girls, as an underpinning to all the other SDGs.

At the same time there has been an increase, especially through social media, in activism and campaigns for the rights and recognition of LGBTQ+ groups and sub groups and most recently, a surge of interest especially from young people, in gender non-binary groups and individuals. In 2011 Rankin and Beemyn, in the United States, uncovered growing gender diversity from their 3,500 surveys and 400 interviews with trans-masculine, trans-feminine and gender-non-conforming people. They found that respondents, especially young people, used more than a hundred different ways to describe their gender identity. Many said describing their gender was not easy, with some resorting to percentages to describe their identities (such as one-third male, one-third female and one-third transgender) and others saying simply, 'I am me'. In the United Kingdom, Bragg et al. (2018) revealed that young people who took part in their study used an 'expanding gender vocabulary' (p. 423) producing at least 23 different terms for gender identities. In her prize-winning novel *Girl, Woman, Other* (Evaristo, 2021), the fictional character Megan/Morgan discovers that the internet contains 'hundreds of genders' describing, with some hilarity, her attempt to navigate this complex world. Relatedly, Josephidou and Bolshaw (2020, p. 3) set out a helpful list of the current common labels that are used to talk about sex and gender in non-binary, non-essentialist ways. Meanwhile a new generation of feminists have engaged with gender theory and activism through social media, and blogs such as 'Feminism 101' which updates feminism for a new generation. The cumulative impact of these gender-focused public and social media debates is a strengthening of a value for regarding gender as socially constructed phenomenon and a strong rejection of gender 'essentialism'.

A trio of recent landmark books, by Fine (2017), Rippon (2019) and Gillies et al. (2017) are worthy of mention at this point as they point out the damaging nature of gender 'essentialism'. The term essentialism implies the belief that a person's gender is innate, 'hard wired', essential in the sense that is part of their essence. Many people hold this belief linking **gender essentialism** to biological differences between males and females. This deeply implicit belief, fostered and perpetuated by our gendered society, implies that society will never succeed in overturning ingrained ideas about the deep rootedness of gender difference. These books have made an important contribution to the gender revolution as they emphasise the enduring dominance of claims about biology and innate gender differences and they reveal the continuing influence of gender binary thinking. Each author demonstrates the power of 'pseudoscience' (Fine, 2017) and 'neurosexism' (Rippon, 2019) to show how a mythology has arisen supporting supposedly 'scientific' arguments to bolster myths about gender differences entailing the forces of genes, neurones and hormones. Gillies et al. (2017) offer an illuminating take on this approach as they show how the Early Years sector is particularly susceptible to arguments that reify science especially neuroscience: 'By adopting the language of neuroscience, early years practitioners can demonstrate knowledge and proficiency' and 'augment the status of their professions' (p. 80).

There is also a huge growth in our awareness and understanding of transgender, a giant step in the direction of a transformation to a less gender-rigid society. Many academics and researchers who work with the concept of gender are now part of an ambitious attempt to transform traditional gender binary thinking into a value for **gender fluidity**. Such people are making a concerted challenge to gender essentialism which implies that a person's gender is fixed in time, unmalleable and impermeable. Relatedly, the very concept of transgender disrupts the crude categories of man/woman; masculinity/femininity and implies a world of gender nuance and variability (Warin & Price, 2020). The children and young people (aged 12–14) who took part in the study by Bragg et al. (2018) cited above included young people who identified with and used 'trans' categories (e.g. gender fluid, agender, non-binary and gender-diverse) (p. 421).

Education and children's well-being

Meanwhile, from another quarter a different and much slower wave of change can also be observed: the gradual emergence of a value for children's well-being and rights. We could first see this coming back in the 1990s with the work of James and Prout (1990) and the announcement of a revolution focused on children's 'voice'. This flow of change has been incredibly slow and has often been impeded altogether for example with the closure of England's **Children's Centres**, fragmentation and privatisation of early childhood education services. However, it has picked up speed recently with the forcefulness of the young climate-changers in their school strikes and prescient activism and their inescapable demand to be heard. This is one area where it is now impossible to ignore the voices of children and young people.

In addition, there has been a growing concern with the emotional well-being of children. This concern has been manifested in two ways. Firstly, the last two decades of schooling have seen several school initiatives focused on providing forms of holistic and emotional support for children and a growing awareness of a need to foster children's emotional literacy (Weare, 2004). A landmark report in 2007 by UNICEF showed how badly we, in the United Kingdom, compared on measures of overall childhood well-being with the 20 other surveyed countries and reminding us that 'The true measure of a nation's standing is how well it attends to its children' (UNICEF, 2007, p. 1). This report caught the public eye and was much discussed in the UK media leading to a growing anxiety from politicians and academics to attend to children's well-being. Partly in response to this national hand-wringing, Layard and Dunn (2009) produced their report for The Children's Society, entitled *A Good Childhood: Searching for Values in a Competitive Age* (with subsequent reports including the most recent in 2021). The title indicated the authors' challenge to the neoliberal school standardisation agenda where educational goals are framed through international competition league table comparisons, and through the pitting of one school against another. This aspect of the educational 'market' was still relatively new at this time with its resultant 'performance culture' where pupils experienced their worth through narrow forms of assessment and examinable academic outcomes. Academics at the time were also aware of a lack of educational purpose (Hayward et al., 2005) and 'a hollow lack of clarity' at the core of educational policy (McLaughlin, 2005) about the purposes of schooling in the United Kingdom. The New Labour government of the millennial years commissioned the Rose report (2009) to examine the state of primary education at the same time as an incredibly thorough independent primary education review was produced by Alexander and colleagues at Cambridge – the Cambridge Review (Alexander, 2010). Both reviews had a new emphasis on children's enjoyment and well-being. However, these reports fared badly and were not able to exert any influence as they were swept aside by the incoming 2010 Coalition government with its renewed emphasis on academic performance especially exams, and a ranking of schools based on the number of GCSE entrants in core subjects.

Dualistic thinking in framing educational purposes: Influences of neoliberalism

Educational sociologists writing about policy during this era described the dualistic thinking that underlined policy and pedagogy. The influence of easily measurable performance goals driven by neoliberal economic competition, and philosophies of personalised teaching derived from child-centred values, was noted as fundamentally incompatible (Biesta, 2014; Shuayb & O'Donnell, 2008). Ball's global review of the preceding 20 years of education policy (2008) revealed that 'Within policy, education is now regarded primarily from an economic point of view' (p. 11). He identified a dualism in schools, an 'institutional schizophrenia' based upon a divide between competing values, between a teacher's own intuitive judgements about good practice and the contrasting demands of standardisation (Ball, 2003, p. 222). Keddie (2016) looked at the influences of neoliberalism on children themselves. She used the term 'children of the market' (p. 109) to describe children's own ideas about purposes of education suggesting, disturbingly, they have become focused entirely on what it means to be 'economically successful'.

The 'well-being' agenda has shifted from an overall concern with children's happiness to a concern for their mental health (DfE, 2017a; NHS Long Term Plan, 2019). In July 2018, the government published health education guidance for schools with mental well-being considered equally important to physical well-being – alongside the new introduction of 'Relationships and Sex Education' (Parkin & Long, 2021). A concern with mental health has been exacerbated in recent times due to the influence of COVID-19 which has shone a light on the exponential growth of minor and major mental health issues in children and young people. A recent report (Lally, 2020) emphasised the influences on strained family relationships, academic stress and reduced contact with friends, alongside a reduction in the services that support children with mental health concerns (CAMHs). Consequently, at the time of writing there is much more government policy noise than previously on the mental health of children and young people.

How far is the Early Years sector subject to the kinds of 'institutional schizophrenia' that Ball identifies? In many ways this sector experiences a much greater degree of freedom from some of the pressures exerted by the influences of neoliberalism. It has always been understood that purposes of care are integrated with the purposes of education for the 3–6-year-old age group. In addition the concept of play, and practices associated with it, soften the performance culture that dominates the education of older age groups. Interestingly, Early Years practitioners sometimes describe their draw to this profession due to its 'low pressure' environment. For example, as part of the research I have undertaken with male teachers in the Early Years (in England, Sweden and Indonesia), I have been told that the attraction to work in this sector is indeed the feeling of freedom that is gained in comparison to the external pressure of teaching older children and young people. In the study I undertook with Swedish male pre-school teachers (described in Warin, 2016), the term 'freedom' was used by all the five men in discussing their values, and their rationales for teaching this particular age group.

However, although the Early Years may be less constrained by an educational performance culture focused on narrow academic achievement, it is increasingly subject to the influences of managerialism based in a neoliberal accountability culture, with an increase in such bureaucratic practices as frequent report writing and documentation (Löfdahl, 2014; Löfgren, 2014). In England Bradbury and Roberts-Holmes (2017) have drawn attention to the ways that schools experience an increasing pressure to contribute to national data required by the schools inspection service (OfSTED) that is aimed at developing the progress, not of the child, but of the school in order to facilitate comparisons between schools. They point out that a school's 'OfSTED story' requires baseline measures for the very young despite differences from the rest of the primary school in terms of **curriculum** and culture (p. 944). Recently, and as a result of neoliberal accountability, and the market driven nature of education, the UK government have just introduced baseline testing in English and Mathematics for 4 year olds. There has been an outcry from early childhood education teachers and parents about this unnecessary and undermining task. For example, Goldstein et al. (2018) pointed out the atmosphere of uncertainty that was created in schools when the plans were announced. The organisation 'More than a Score' actively campaigned against this plan and attracted 700 experts to back up their resistance in an open letter to the **DfE** describing the plan as both pointless and damaging. Recent critiques have been offered by Robert-Holmes and Moss (2021) and Blanco-Bayo (2022). Despite the resistance, baseline testing is now statutory for children starting their 'reception' year in school.

The resistance to this last imposition of a damaging measurement culture on the very young has perhaps intensified a shift towards the well-being pole of 'institutional schizophrenia'. COVID-19 has reinforced this further. A possible silver lining is that the education of young children may now be based on a deeper attention to children's own agency, a willingness to hear their voices about their education and a recognition that pre-school and school are for making friends, managing social relationships and having fun. However, anecdotal accounts from Early Years teacher friends suggest that this optimistic view is far from being realised. Although the new Early Years Foundation Statge (**EYFS**) curriculum appears to lessen staff workload through minimising written observations, there is still enormous pressure from OfSTED and in DfE guidance to devote much time on evidence collection demonstrating children's progression.

Early Years educators have always had a deep concern with young children's social and emotional well-being and have understood their pedagogic purposes to be equally focused on helping children to manage and maximise their social relationships as much as to develop their capacity for literacy and numeracy. Indeed, in this respect, education policy and practice for older students (including HE) has much to learn from the Early Years.

I have discussed two significant societal changes that concern the childhood and education of our young children: the gender revolution, the turn to children's social and emotional well-being. When these transformative waves merge there is the potential for a sea-change in the world of gender and early childhood education, a combination of gender-fluidity and an elevation of children and young people. In my own country, and the world over, we need to raise the status of early childhood education and, at the same time, create social environments that celebrate gender fluid thinking. A way to operationalise this combined purpose is to make use of the concept of a gender flexible pedagogy.

Spotlight on Theory: Locating This Concept in Wider Theories of Gender

The identification of, and promotion of, a gender flexible pedagogy is based on an understanding of sociological gender-focused theory that relies on interweaving several older, deeper and more basic theories. I would like to peel back some of the theoretical assumptions that lie underneath the superficial presentation of a gender flexible pedagogy. So this section will be rather like peeling back the layers of skin in an onion, where the outermost layer, a 'gender flexible pedagogy', has an inner theoretical core (Figure 1.1).

So let us regard the outermost layer as a gender flexible pedagogy. We then peel back to see the deeper influencing layers; **queer theory**; **intersectionality**; **feminist poststructuralism**; the social construction of gender – at the core.

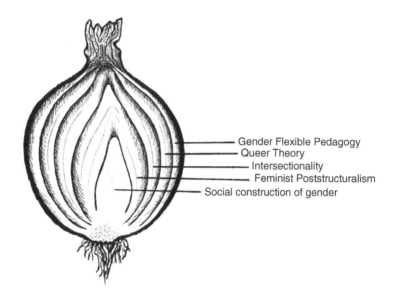

Gender Flexible Pedagogy
Queer Theory
Intersectionality
Feminist Poststructuralism
Social construction of gender

Figure 1.1 Onion diagram – illustration by Anna Warin

Queer theory

The layer of onion beneath the outer skin is Queer Theory, a powerful theory for linking current thinking about gender and sexuality together with broader ideas about the situated and plural nature of identity. This approach has the explanatory power to disrupt the gender binary of male/female and closely related binaries such as masculine/feminine and heterosexual/homosexual.

The word 'queer' has several meanings and was originally, of course, used in a pejorative way, in its sense as 'peculiar' (odd, different) as a form of homophobic slur. However, another use of the word, especially when used as a verb, means to spoil or ruin something – to disrupt. In this sense it is akin to Butler's idea about 'troubling' or disrupting gender (1999). It is used to signal a deconstruction of the crude but well-established boundary between gender and sexuality binaries that are constructed through our binary language system (Jagose, 1996). The word has been reclaimed by LGBTQ+ activists and theorists as a positive theory with related activity to describe the intention to break down boundaries that are drawn too rigidly and that are based on essentialist categories. It is doubly powerful because it is simultaneously the word that often implies the LGBTQ+ community, and also implies a rejection of boundaries between norm-based categories. Queer has become a powerful verb signalling gender non-conformity at the same time as portraying a radical approach to tired old monolithic theoretical categories.

One such monolith is the concept of identity. Queer theory challenges the concept of identity as something that is fixed and necessary. It 'aims to subvert the entire concept of identity' (Thurer, 2005, p. 99) by emphasising the fluid, dynamic and constructed nature of identities. It breaks down the idea that a person's gender and sexuality are fixed within their biological, sexed body, so it is an approach that emphasises the 'multiplicities of gender' and the 'pluralities of sexuality' (Robinson & Diaz, 2006) which in turn leads to a deconstruction of the gender binary. It challenges the taken-for-granted positioning of heterosexuality as the dominant sexuality and draws attention to the ways that non-heterosexual identities are 'othered'.

Intersectionality

It is impossible to ignore the identity essentialism of approaches to race and ethnicity as well as gender, especially since the escalation of 'Black Lives Matter' following the death of George Floyd in 2020. So, peeling back another layer of the theoretical onion, we find a deeper layer that asks us to question our treatment of gender as an independent social category and that highlights the crosscutting nature of social categories. This kind of theoretical questioning is known as **intersectionality** and is increasingly recognised and valued as a way of expressing flexible and fluid (and non-fixed) theories of identity. Valocchi (2005) hails queer analysis for its capacity to attend to intersectionality 'the crosscutting identifications of individuals along several axes of social difference' (p. 754). Identity theories that are based on an intersectional awareness draw on the feminist body of work represented by Crenshaw (2017) and others who identified the limitations of homogenous, tightly bounded, identity categories and who revealed the interweaving of different dimensions of difference such as class, race, ethnicity, age, nation, together with gender. Such theorists pointed out the restrictions of identity-based analyses and emphasised the analytic importance of intersectionality.

Poststructuralist theories (and their natural alliance with queer theory; transgender)

Poststructuralist theories of gender and identity are aligned with queer theory sharing an intention to break down boundaries that are drawn too tightly and that are based on essentialist categories. Josephidou and Bolshaw (2020) define post-structuralism as a theory that 'problematises the idea that the "truth" is knowable', often seeking to disrupt that which is *seen* to be true' a definition based on Mukherji and Albon (2009, p. 31). The poststructuralist approach has challenged traditional psychological theories of identity which have always emphasised the unified and individualistic nature of self (see Warin, 2010). Many feminists have embraced poststructuralism because this underpinning intention to deconstruct boundaries is directed at gender-focused binaries in particular. MacNaughton (2000) is a strong proponent of feminist poststructuralist approaches to gender and especially to gender in early childhood education. She interprets young children's gender-based practices as:

> ways of being gendered that do not regulate but are *full of possibilities* for girls, for boys and for their teachers. These possibilities will always express a complexity of social relations and social practices. They will not be static or fixed but an expression of constantly negotiated meanings and relationships. (p. 3)

Her approach reminds us that identities, including gendered identities, are produced within and through social relationships. This means that they are fluid, ever-changing and not fixed. What is more, this approach acknowledges that social contexts are always composed of power dynamics between the participating players. An early feminist poststructuralist, Walkerdine, wrote a classic paper (1981) describing identity in a poststructuralist way as 'a nexus of subjectivities, in relations of power which are constantly shifting' (p. 14). Feminist poststructuralist approaches are tuned into sociolinguistics, recognising how power is exercised particularly through language. Binaries such as male/female, adult/child, heterosexual/homosexual are imbued with power relations. They 'operate to constitute and perpetuate artificial hierarchical relations of power between the paired concepts, which are perceived as polarised opposites' (Robinson & Diaz, 2006, p. 40).

A challenge to the dominance of gender binary thinking is also emerging from recent sociological studies into the upbringing of children who are gender non-conforming.

> Gender variance exposes the limits of the gender binary and the overly deterministic role it ascribes to assigned sex, in turn signalling possibilities for social change against dominant ideologies and practices. (Rahilly, 2015, p. 339)

The significance of transgender identity is not new within debates about gender. For example Halberstam's influential book on female masculinity (1998) supports the idea that masculinity does not reduce down to the male body – and femininity to the female body. However an interest in transgender is developing apace in many countries such as the United States, where Rahilly's studies were located and in the new academic discipline of transgender studies (Martino & Cumming-Potvin, 2020). Pre-school managers and practitioners are becoming alert to the possibilities of transgender, in its various manifestations, including possibilities for children who feel 'trapped in the wrong body' and children who want to play with the possibility of different gender identities. As Vollans (2016) points out in her article for pre-school practitioners, transgender can be seen 'as a challenge to the certainty and rigidity of the categories male and female – trans is a challenge to this and an escape from it' (p. 31).

We have seen how the theories promoted through feminist poststructuralism, expanded by queer theorists and advocates of transgender, add up to a dismantling of the gender binary.

The theoretical core of the onion: The social construction of gender

At the heart of the theoretical layers I have identified lies the idea that gender is a socially constructed phenomenon. It is not innate. We make it up. It is not 'an absolute truth that exists but rather an understanding of how people choose, or are obliged, to act in specific gendered ways' (Josephidou & Bolshaw, 2020, p. 3). Butler's concept of performativity (1990) challenges gender as a fixed identity and draws attention to the ways that gender is not only constructed but is performed and 'fabricated' in acts and gestures (1999, p. 173). Her work rests on the understanding that gender identities are socially situated, a point which she expands to argue that the practices of self-presentation bring about the creation of gender identities.

For those new to theorising about gender, the above section may seem a little overwhelming. So let me reduce this to a couple of related statements that sum up key principles to take forward as you read the rest of this book.

- Gender is something that we make up and perform. It is not innate, biologically determined or God-given.
- This means that we can construct it differently and perform it differently. We can change our thinking. We can do this in way that benefits individuals and society at large by removing our made-up gender boundaries, constraints and binaries.

These points mean that we can develop gender flexibility and that teachers in particular, specifically Early Years teachers, have a crucial role in delivering a 'gender flexible pedagogy', which I now elaborate more precisely.

The Concept of a Gender Flexible Pedagogy

In order to explain what I mean by this concept, I want to talk first about the 'gender flexible' element and then about the '**pedagogy**' part of this term.

I have chosen the term 'gender flexibility' to identify my approach to the transformation that I see as necessary and the potential for change in early childhood education. Yet there are some closely related terms that are beginning to be pervasive in current discussions of gender such as 'gender fluidity', 'gender neutrality' and '**gender sensitivity**'. So I'll just take a moment to explain my own take on the differences and my preference for 'gender flexibility'.

I find that the term gender-neutral can imply a disregard for gender – a kind of **gender blindness** or lack of gender awareness. I was interested, and impressed, to see that the brilliant TV documentary on the subject of gender in the primary school used the title 'gender free' rather than gender neutral. Produced in 2018 to much acclaim it was entitled *No More Boys and Girls: Can Our Kids Go Gender Free?* (will be referred to again in this book). The preferred term 'gender free' suggests a consciousness of the influence of gender in young children's lives and a wish to free ourselves from it. Whereas 'gender neutral' implies a pretence that gender does not exist as the incredibly influential social construction that we all, to a greater or lesser extent, collude in perpetuating.

Gender sensitivity is an extremely useful term which describes a goal of gender consciousness or gender awareness. I prefer it to the term gender awareness as the emphasis on sensitivity suggests that nuances are possible. A person might be a little gender aware in some contexts, highly conscious of gender in others and perhaps somewhat insensitive in others. Sensitivity suggests the position that we can actually learn and develop through the right kinds of sensitisation interventions. Gender sensitivity is the opposite of 'gender blindness', which is a disregard for the importance of gender as a mediating influence in social interactions.

Gender fluidity is also a very rich term which has uses beyond the realm of education and schooling. It challenges gender 'essentialism' suggesting gender is not fixed but is instead a free-flowing experience which changes from one context to another and will change within a person's lifespan, changeable across time and place. Butler's words elaborate the concept nicely where she describes gender as a 'free-floating artifice'. She goes on to explain that the categories '*man* and *masculine* might just as easily signify a female body as a male one, and *woman* and *feminine* a male body as easily as a female one' (Butler, 1990, p. 6). We can see that gender fluidity is closely aligned to queer and poststructuralist theories. It has also been adopted as a relevant term to emphasise gender non-conformity and transgender.

Gender flexibility is particularly useable within an educational context especially one where gender-sensitive staff can make conscious choices to challenge traditional gender stereotypes within their own behaviours, appearance choices and performances in front of children and in the resources and activities they create with and for them. The term gender flexibility arose from data I collected at **Acorns** pre-school (Warin, 2018), a setting that had an unusually high proportion of male practitioners. (I will be demonstrating how this term actually works in practice and drawing on this case study in Chapter 5.) Gender flexibility links to the idea of the versatile, child-centred, pre-school teacher. Just as athletes train their bodies for flexibility, pre-school teachers can train themselves to perform versatile roles and activities.

So, in a nutshell, making sense of these terms and the relationships between them, I suggest that:

Gender neutrality is equated with gender blindness and is a misleading term for identifying the kinds of positive gender transformation we might hope to see in society. Gender sensitivity is vital and implies a necessary first step to the development of a more gender fluid society, a liberating way to conceptualise gender freedom from gender essentialism. In the context of school, staff can strategically practice gender flexibility and encourage children to do so. In the pre-school, gender flexibility is part of a pre-school teacher's versatility as they respond to the varied needs of children.

And now for pedagogy. The term is in wide usage amongst those familiar with the world of education where it delineates an academic discipline. However, it is not part of everyday language so apologies to the educators whilst I briefly explain it, and argue for its value. It is sometimes used quite simply as a synonym for 'teaching' but it is more than this (and hence my reason for integrating it into my concept of a gender flexible pedagogy) as it implies an *approach* to teaching (defined as such in Wikipedia, 2022). It suggests an underpinning philosophy of teaching, based on theories of teaching and learning, as well as a set of practices. So it implies both what is taught and how it is taught: the behaviours, practices and disposition of the teacher and the learning experiences, resources, activities they place in front of the learner. The concept of pedagogy merits further discussion and is a focus of Chapter 4. So, overall, a gender flexible pedagogy is an approach that allows for principles of gender-flexibility to be practiced by the teacher within their teaching practices and underlying beliefs.

Turning Theory Into Practice to Develop a Gender Flexible Pedagogy

You may have read the above statements about gender flexibility, and associated terms, with a degree of critical cynicism and thought to yourself 'Hmm. Easier said than done!' You would be right. It is certainly easy to say and incredibly challenging to do; to change our deeply ingrained gendered ways of thinking that have been developed over centuries. We have to begin by developing gender-sensitive antennae which pick up on our own behaviours and language practices and which hone in on the gendered practices of others around us. Two nice examples illustrate what I mean by this.

In my own life as a parent, I noticed that I frequently referred to my two male children as 'the boys' when I was talking about them or to them. Why did I need to draw attention to their gender in this way? I noticed other parents similarly clustering children by gender when referring to them. Although most gender-enlightened teachers now no longer undertake the old-fashioned practice of lining children up in separate gender groups (although see Chapter 7), there are many more subtle ways of reinforcing and entrenching gender difference by simply referring, quite unnecessarily, to gender group membership as in the instruction to a group of boys 'Boys, please tidy up now'.

In the brilliant TV documentary, referred to above, *Can Our Children Go Gender Free?*, a primary school class teacher, Graham Andre, is made aware that he uses affectionate terms when addressing the girls which he does not use with boys. Children in the class are tasked with catching him out every time he does this resulting, of course, in entertaining TV. This is the kind of subtle language practice that we need to become aware of and then 'catch ourselves out' every time we slip into these habits. So the first step to be taken in order to turn theory into practice is to develop gender-sensitive antennae.

How This Book Can Be Used

The book incorporates various pedagogical features such as case studies, stories about innovative practices, interview extracts and international comparisons. Each chapter will end with one or two reflective questions and also with the novel feature of a 'Reader Challenge'. Whilst these hopefully make for an engaging reading experience for individuals, they can also be useful for groups within a professional setting or with friends and family.

The case study material and illustrative stories are based on the many years I have spent researching gender in education. I have now produced an internationally recognised body of research about men's participation as teachers in early childhood education and care. Of relevance to the theme of this book, my research career has taken me through research on:

- young children's construction of gender identities;
- research on family gender roles;
- an investigation of Swedish male pre-school teachers, referred to in this book as the **Swedish study**;
- an ethnographic case study of an English pre-school with a high proportion of male staff, referred to here as the **Acorns study**;
- a large-scale study of the recruitment and practices of male teachers in pre-school – the **GenderEYE project**.

Through various research publications, I have argued for and evidenced the concept of a gender flexible pedagogy: gender-sensitive teachers delivering a gender-sensitive curriculum.

A word about the terminology associated with early years sector

As I have developed as a teacher, researcher and academic within the English education system, the phrase 'Early Years' trips of my tongue as the familiar signifier of the educational phase that is provided for young children in this country. It is usually understood to cover the 0–5 years provision of professional support for young and very young children and babies. In other countries this phrase is not used and is not so intelligible internationally. Comparable descriptors are 'Early Years education' (**EYE**) and 'early childhood education' (ECE). In a recent international collaborative book on the topic of men's career trajectories as practitioners within this educational sector (Brody et al., 2021), the large international authorial team, which included myself, decided to use the term 'early childhood education and care' and its widely recognised acronym **ECEC**. Here, as indicated in the title of this book I will adopt the term 'early childhood education' as it has the advantage of being somewhat shorter and also very widely used on an international scale. However, the reader will find that the acronym **ECEC** occurs in some of the quotations from other academics writing about the early childhood education sector.

The structure of this book

This is informed by its aim of explaining, illustrating and promoting the concept of a gender flexible pedagogy. This is managed by responding to three key questions about the nature of this principle: what, who and how:

> **What** is a gender flexible pedagogy?
> **Who** is implicated in delivering a gender flexible pedagogy?
> **How** can it be put into practice?

These questions frame the book structure by diving it into three sections.

Following this **Introduction** (Chapter 1), Chapters 2 and 3 form **Section I** and they examine the 'what' question by asking what is the content of a gender flexible pedagogy? How is it implemented in terms of curriculum? How does it impact on activities and provision of resources? Chapter 2 invites the reader to consider what curriculum means, who decides on it and what place gender has within it. Chapter 3 focuses on resources and activities for the early years which enable gender flexibility and help to 'smash stereotypes'.

The 'who' of gender flexible pedagogy is the concern of **Section II**, in Chapters 4 and 5. These concern key questions about the nature of the Early Years workforce: How Early Years practitioners are qualified and how they experience the rewards and challenges of the job. Chapter 4 discusses concerns about the diversity of the workforce and the recruitment of, and support for, under-represented groups. Chapter 5 highlights the versatility and flexibility necessary for a job in the early years. It draws on research about who does what within the Early Years setting and how gender mediates the allocation of roles.

Chapters 6 and 7 then form **Section III** and are focused on a discussion of 'how' the principle of gender flexible pedagogy may be promoted and practiced. Chapter 6 examines how gender impacts on relationships in the Early Years setting: peer relationships; adult/child relationships/staff team dynamics; the interaction between the ECE setting and its wider community of families. Chapter 7 examines the idea of gender sensitivity training and **unconscious gender bias**. It pays special attention to the importance of leadership in Early Years settings as way to establish a gender flexible pedagogy.

The book's **Conclusion**, **Section IV**, Chapter 8, crystallises the preceding discussion into a set of practical suggestions about the **what**, **who** and **how** of gender flexibility in ECE. It will position the potential contribution of a gender flexible pedagogy within the bigger transformative project of weakening the gender binary.

Finally, I end this introduction by encouraging you to take up the call to develop a gender flexible pedagogy. Read. Absorb. Discuss. Let this book help you to develop the gender-sensitive antennae that is vital if we are to help each other break down society's rigid and constraining gender binaries that reproduce the old gender order and perpetuate gender inequalities and injustices.

Section I

What Is a Gender Flexible Pedagogy?

2

Curriculum Matters: The 'What' of a Gender Flexible Pedagogy

Introduction

What is the content of a **gender flexible pedagogy**? What kinds of choices would gender flexible teachers need to make about *what* to teach? In this chapter, we ask how far 'stereotype smashing' is on or off the menu in Early Years settings. I've adopted this catchy term, which is used by several gender-focused organisations including the campaign recently mounted by British Science week to change perceptions about employees in Science, Technology, Engineering and Mathematics (STEM). This chapter includes discussion about the Early Years Foundation Stage (**EYFS**) in the United Kingdom, and the place of gender within it. I make comparisons with other countries where there is an explicit aim to 'challenge **gender stereotypes**'.

The chapter is divided into four sections. Firstly, I suggest we think about what the term **curriculum** means which entails some consideration of the concept of knowledge and how it is influenced by political concerns about who decides what kinds of knowledge matter. Then we go on to consider what this means for young children through an investigation of international curricula guidance for the Early Years sector, examining some models of good practice. Next the chapter discusses the implications of burying a gender focus within more general guidance about the promotion of diversity culture. Next, I give some thought to the changing nature of curricula over time with attention to newer priorities such as outdoor education where it is important for practitioners to develop and sustain their gender-sensitive antennae. Finally, I offer some conclusions and suggest that gender should be clearly and visibly part of the Early Years menu if we are to develop a gender flexible pedagogy in the Early Years.

What Is Curriculum?

So firstly: What is curriculum and how relevant is it to the concept of a gender-flexible pedagogy? In the paragraph above I used the term 'menu' to describe the curriculum. This is useful as a metaphor for the assortment of offerings that can be provided for young children. There are a multitude of other definitions. Indeed, Thijs and Van DenAkker (2009, p. 9) tell us that there are as many definitions of the term 'curriculum' as there are authors. They favour a very short definition of curriculum as a *plan for learning*, reflected in many languages, including the classical Dutch term *leerplan*, the German *Lehrplan* and the Swedish *läroplan*. This simple definition allows for 'all sorts of elaboration for specific curricular levels, contexts and representations' (Thijs & Van Den Akker, 2009, p. 9).

With older children the word 'curriculum' often signals quite specific content. Another word 'syllabus' comes to mind here too which tends to signify the subject matter or content of a specific subject area such as Mathematics, English or Physics whilst 'curriculum' is a more general term, and often implies an overview by government as in a 'National Curriculum'. Of most relevance to the Early Years, Colwell (2015), in the book *Reflective Teaching for the Early Years*, takes a curriculum definition from the National Council for Curriculum and Assessment (2004, p. 2) who refer to the provision of 'learning experiences... formal or informal, planned or unplanned, which contribute to the child's development'.

Who decides on curriculum? This is a tricky question as it concerns issues over the control of 'knowledge' and values that are deemed important at different school levels. It is a political question as it implicates questions about power and control. How far a country's government should be involved in determining the curriculum is a particularly vexed question, which I shall turn to next as I consider the politics of curriculum.

The politics of curriculum

In the United Kingdom there was no national curriculum (NC) before 1988. For many readers the era that existed prior to the introduction of the NC may seem like the Dark Ages but I recall these days very well because I trained to be a teacher in the late 1970s. In those days the curriculum was dictated by the public exam system which assessed a syllabus prescribed by the exam boards. In subjects that were not examined teachers were relatively free to devise their own curricula (I taught Drama before there was a Drama GCSE). In my period of initial teacher training, we had it drummed into us that the content of our teaching would be based on clear aims and objectives and these, in turn, should be based on pupil interests, individually and collectively, which we would take the trouble to find out by talking with pupils and with their parents. I was part of a teacher uproar when the national curriculum was first introduced because it had arrived out a mistrust of teachers' professional abilities and also a view of knowledge that many of us considered to be elitist. I realised then that curricula decisions are political because they are based on a view about what counts as knowledge and who gets to control knowledge.

There is much debate about how far governments should impose prescriptive curriculum content and what that content should be. These debates have increasingly included the Early Years sector where they have focused on concerns about time allocated to play and time allocated to 'school readiness' activities especially numeracy and literacy. At secondary school level they have been played out in the setting of curricula for older children and especially within the high-profile areas of 'knowledge' content that is assessed in public exams such as the exams that are taken at age 16 (in the United Kingdom this is the General Certificate of Secondary Education [GCSE]). Termed 'knowledge wars' (Wilby, 2018), this perennial debate is not only about what should be taught, and who gets to decide, but is also about the very nature of knowledge. In the United Kingdom, it has focused on the difference between knowledge which is powerful and knowledge that is possessed by the powerful (Wilby, 2018; Young, 1971). In 2008, Michael Young produced a controversial book called *Bringing Knowledge Back In* arguing that English children and young people should have access to 'powerful knowledge', knowledge from the traditional academic disciplines, as opposed to 'everyday knowledge'. However, his concept of powerful knowledge is deeply flawed as it pre-supposes that there is a fixed body of knowledge that can be readily absorbed by all children and young people regardless of their cultures, communities and backgrounds. Young's ideas about high status knowledge were translated into policy by Michael Gove (UK Education Minister from 2010 to 2014) who believed that the teaching force was infested by left wing ideologues who held an 'anti-knowledge culture'. Gove attempted to prescribe the specific syllabus for the GCSE English Literature causing deep antagonism amongst teachers who saw this as an undermining of their professionalism. His choices were based on assumptions about the value of a classic, white middle class selection of English literature: prescribing the study of authors such as the English poets: Byron, and Keats, and English novelists, Austen, Dickens and Hardy. His reforms led to a very narrow academic idea of knowledge and most importantly a view of knowledge that was elitist and white. This kind of government prescription raises the unsettling sense that teachers are not to be trusted and it also raises deeper underlying questions about what passes for knowledge. Significantly, it makes no attempt to include children's own views either through direct consultation with children and young people or via teacher insights into their interests.

We now reflect on how these questions about knowledge and power play out in the context of early childhood education?

What Does Curriculum Mean for Young Children?

Colwell (2015, p. 196) points out that 'A curriculum for younger children is a relatively new phenomenon'. She, and her team of co-authors, provide a historical overview of how a curriculum for Early Years has developed in the United Kingdom. They track the Early Years curriculum from the time of the famous Plowden report in 1967, which was the first mention of provision for the Early Years, to the Rumbold report in 1990 which addressed concerns about the patchiness of quality, through to the 2008 introduction of the EYFS which included principles for children aged 0–5 and which combined principles of both education and care and also advocated a play-based curriculum.

Early Childhood Education (ECE) is much less in the public eye than educational sectors for older children and young people. The relative invisibility of ECE is a double-edged sword. It creates the greater 'freedom' which is sometimes identified as a reason for choosing the profession of Early Years teaching (as we have seen) but also creates the lower status of this work which implies a lower value for the care and education of young children compared to older students. In the early years of education, the low status has made for less prescription from national and local governing bodies – until recently. However, the relative freedoms of the Early Years phase in England have been disrupted through the introduction of 'base line assessment' which will be discussed shortly. A further reason for the relative lack of government prescription (or interference) is that an overly controlled and overly specific curriculum runs counter to the strong principle of child-centredness which underlies so many pedagogies and plans for early childhood education in England and elsewhere.

Xu and colleagues have undertaken a systematic review of the **ECE** curricula of 18 different countries and present commonalities in their report (Xu et al., 2020a). A general observation is that most countries have some kind of national curriculum for the Early Years. For example Xu's comparison of 18 different curricula comes to the conclusion that 'a 0–5/6 curriculum framework that supports children's care and education in the early years of life prior to formal primary schooling appears to be a global trend' (Xu et al., 2020, p. 27). The review also draws out the pervasive principle of child-centredness especially in national curriculum expressions about the value of the 'unique child'.

In England, the country where I live and work, there has been a recent re-visitation of the **EYFS** for children aged 0–5, the national curriculum for this sector (DfE, 2021b). One of the most significant changes, which has attracted much public debate, is the mandatory assessment of 4-year-olds, discussed for several years and now compulsory. There has been an outcry from Early Years teachers who feel their work is misunderstood and undervalued and from educators who see the baseline assessment as a 'simplistic reductionism' which serves neoliberal political agendas but does not have the child's best interests at heart (Roberts-Holmes & Bradbury, 2017). On the positive side the new version of the EYFS is attempting to signal less prescriptive guidance than before. It distinguishes between elements of young children's care and education that are mandatory and elements where teachers may exercise their professional judgement and where they are free to respond to the needs of their communities and individual children. For example:

> 1.8. The ELGs [Early Learning Goals] should not be used as a curriculum or in any way to limit the wide variety of rich experiences that are crucial to child development.
>
> 1.9. Instead the ELGs should support teachers to make a holistic best-fit judgment about the child. (DfE, 2021b, p. 11)

However, the mandatory assessment regulations undermine this less prescriptive tone. The 'feel' of the document makes an interesting contrast with the equivalent documents in other countries as the overall tone is one of legislative compunction which positions teachers as undependable and children as extremely vulnerable. There is less emphasis on play than formerly and there is much strong guidance on safeguarding. The document emphasises 'school readiness', and assessments to enable this, with a firm eye to the child's future performance as a contributor to national educational performance. There is no mention of gender and little atten- tion to wider goals of diversity and equality.

What Place Does Gender Have Within the ECE Curriculum?

In 2012, I spoke with pre-school practitioners in Sweden as part of a study about the presence of male teachers within the Early Years workforce there (Warin, 2016). We discussed how far they aimed to challenge gender roles with the children, and I was impressed that they described conscious stereotype-smashing practices. I was also struck by their ready familiarity with their Early Years curriculum, quoting 'The pre-school should counteract traditional gender patterns and gender roles'

(Skolverket, 2010, p. 4). Since this experience, I have been interested to see how explicit gender is on the menu in other countries.

In writing this chapter, I have drawn on the systematic comparison of international curricula undertaken by Xu and colleagues (2020) which includes relevant content on the positioning of gender in a more general comparison of statements about diversity and equality. I also undertook my own informal survey of the ECE curricula in various different countries, for the purposes of writing this book. I draw on both these surveys to compare and contrast the positioning of gender as a topic for inclusion within national documents that outline guidance for the young.

The review by Xu et al. of Early Childhood Education and Care (**ECEC**) national curricula in 18 countries concludes that gender equality and diversity:

> seems to be an under-addressed aspect among international ECEC frameworks. Although the majority mention gender alongside other aspects of equality and diversity when claiming inclusion of all children, few expands on it or details any practical guidance. (Xu et al., 2020, p. 37)

Xu et al. note three exceptions – the NC frameworks of Northern Ireland, Sweden and Taiwan. These authors conclude that despite the existence of some exemplary national curricular guidance there is no mention in any frameworks of challenging the **gender binary** and dualism as advocated by various gender researchers such as Nolan and Raban (2015) and Xu et al. (2020b). However, the Icelandic document may be an exception here as, unusually, it draws attention to theoretical approaches that value the deconstruction of the gender binary, pointing out that:

> it is reasonable for schools to make use of the knowledge that has been acquired in new studies, such as gender studies, **queer theory**, multicultural studies and disability studies. (Icelandic National Curriculum, 2022, p. 19)

My own informal survey elicited relevant information from: Norway, Sweden, China, South Africa, Ireland, Germany, United States (New York), Australia, Iceland and Indonesia. I made use of my network of international Early Years colleagues many of whom I have come to know through the activities of the Early Childhood Educational Research Association (**EECERA**) especially the EECERA SIG on Gender Balance in ECE and the collaboration many of us undertook in a co-edited book about the presence of male teachers in ECE (Brody et al., 2021). I posed two questions to my contacts in these countries:

- Are there explicit statements in (name of country) curriculum documents for ECE about gender such as challenging gender stereotypes/teaching about gender?
- Are there some broader statements that relate to diversity, equality and inclusion?

I found the following pattern across these ten countries (Table 2.1):

Table 2.1 Centrality of gender on the ECE curricula of ten different countries

Centrality of gender in NC	Countries
Specific guidance on gender	Sweden, Iceland, Ireland
Gender within broader diversity guidance	Germany, South Africa, Norway
No mention of gender	China, Indonesia, United States (New York state), Australia

3 countries mention gender specifically.

3 countries mention gender as part of a broader diversity focus.

4 countries make no mention at all.

Table 2.1 is inevitably a rather crude depiction of a much more complex picture. For example, early childhood education documents in Ireland are very detailed with regard to diversity and equality and give some quite precise guidance about gender although there is no discrete section on gender as such (Síolta: The National Quality Framework for Early Childhood Education, and Aistear: The Curriculum Framework for Early Childhood, 2022). I have included it in the category 'specific guidance on gender' because of the level of detail. Germany does not have a national curriculum for ECE as education is regulated on federal state level in Germany. At this level there are 'orientation plans' and 'educational programs' (which can be interpreted as curriculum). Gender is not mentioned at all in some German states. However, in Bavaria there is a whole chapter on the topic which runs to several pages and makes some very concrete recommendations (personal correspondence with Tim Rohrmann). In South Africa there is no specific mention of gender as a discrete social category for policy aims. However, the National Curriculum Statement Grades R-12 (p. 5) is sensitive to issues of diversity such as poverty, inequality, race, gender, language, age, disability and other factors. In Australia, there is nothing specifically about combating gender hierarchy. Diversity is usually focused on culture, ability and first nations peoples (personal correspondence with Victoria Sullivan).

Between the Xu et al. survey and my own survey, there appear to be only five countries that have an explicit and detailed statement about the need to focus on gender: Northern Ireland, Sweden, Taiwan, Iceland and Ireland. Exemplary statements come from Iceland and Sweden as set out in the box below. The Swedish statement is from the most recent version of the curriculum guidance as opposed to the 2010 version quoted above and incorporates a 'stereotype smashing' statement articulated as a duty to 'combat gender patterns'. As we have seen Iceland's guidance also includes an encouragement for practitioners to be aware of 'new studies' on gender such as **queer theory**.

Case study

Exemplary statements from Iceland and Sweden on gender within the Early Years curriculum

Iceland

The Icelandic document quotes the country's *Act on Equal Status and Equal Rights of Women and Men, No. 10/2008,* (amended in 2011) which has clear provisions that:

> at all school levels [including preschool] pupils should be educated in equal rights where an effort should be made to prepare both genders for equal participation in society, both in family life and on the labour market. Emphasis should be on boys and girls having as extensive and as equal opportunities as possible. Nowhere in school activities, content, or in working methods should there be any obstacles for either gender. It is important that all school activities, both in classes as in all communication, should be guided by these provisions of the Equality Act. (p. 19)

Sweden

In Sweden, the Curriculum for Preschool (Skolverket, 2021) states that:

> The preschool should actively and consciously promote the equal rights and opportunities of all children, regardless of gender. The preschool also has a responsibility to combat gender patterns that limit children's development, choices and learning. How the preschool organises education, how children are treated and what demands and expectations are made of children all contribute to shaping their perceptions of what is female and what is male. The preschool should therefore organise education so that children mix, play and learn together, and test and develop their abilities and interests, with the same opportunities and on equal terms, regardless of gender. (Skolverket, 2021, p. 7)

Critical question

Which are the most powerful phrases (in both statements) for promoting a gender flexible pedagogy?

Diversity Guidance, Intersectionality and the Positioning of Gender

Despite the absence of specific gender-focused statements, many national curriculum statements for the early years of education state strong aims about diversity, equality and inclusion. The United Nations Convention on the Rights of the Child (UNICEF, 1989) has made a major impact in this respect. This is a universally agreed set of non-negotiable standards and obligations founded on respect for the dignity and worth of each child, regardless of race, colour, gender, language, religion, opinions, origins, wealth, birth status or ability. The curriculum survey by Xu et al. (2020) demonstrates the prevalence of broad statements about equality, diversity and inclusion (EDI).

> Aspects concerning equality and diversity of children and their families/ communities are multiple. They include but are not limited to: abilities and needs, culture, gender, ethnicity, race, language, sexual orientation, religion, and socio-economic status. All frameworks require that ECEC (early childhood education and care) curricula take those differences into account and act against discrimination of any forms. (p. 35)

There are many excellent presentations of the values of diversity, equality and inclusion now enshrined in statements about underlying values and principles for pre-school. For example Norway's Framework Plan for Kindergartens (2021, p. 10) has the following under a heading 'Equity and Equality':

> Kindergartens shall promote equity and equality irrespective of gender, functional ability, sexual orientation, gender identity and expression, ethnicity, culture, social status, language, religion and world view. Kindergartens shall combat all forms of discrimination and promote compassion. Kindergartens shall base their activities on the principle of equality and anti- discrimination and help to ensure that the children are able to experience and create an egalitarian society.

How much should gender be specified in curriculum statements?

A central question for discussion is whether it is preferable to have gender-focused goals within a broader agenda for equality, diversity and inclusion? Or alternatively whether gender needs an explicit focus on the curriculum in order for Early Years practitioners to take it seriously.

There are arguments for and against the specific mention of gender. The argument for articulating wider goals of diversity and inclusion which *include* gender is that this represents an intersectional approach where all forms of inclusion/ exclusion and diversity issues apply to the whole range of social difference categories (such as race, religion, age, gender, social class and others) and can also allow for their intersections rather than treating these as discrete difference categories.

However, these broad statements about diversity can come across as very bland, rhetorical or abstract and seem difficult to apply to everyday classroom life. As one of my contacts wrote about the ECE curriculum in her country (Australia): 'Although there are a lot of pretty words that could be taken to include gender, it's not really a focus'. This observation typifies the general trend. Cover-all EDI statements can also downplay the importance of the individual categories of gender, and other social difference categories such as race. For example, whilst the Swedish curriculum has the best and most detailed exposition of attention to gender, some have pointed out that it has a history of racial blindness (Konde, 2017).

The rhetorical blandness of NC statements about diversity can actually mask discriminatory practices. There is a nice example from Kopo kindergarten in Indonesia that illustrates how diversity principles, articulated in the setting's rhetoric (mission statement), are put into practice (Adriany & Warin, 2014). We can see that a broad emphasis on diversity can perpetuate a form of **gender blindness** in this case.

Case study

Diversity: Rhetoric and practice in an Indonesian preschool (adapted from Adriany & Warin, 2014, p. 323)

Vina Adriany undertook an ethnographic study of a pre-school setting, Kopo kinder-garten, in the city of Bandung, Indonesia, with a focus on gender relations. Her findings showed how the school demonstrated a strong value for children's individual diversities as part of the school's child-centred philosophy, with each child perceived as a unique individual. This is apparent in her field notes about the school's annual musical drama where the diversity goal was prominent. She tells the story of how the pre-school planned and enacted a fantasy tale, important within the country's culture.

The story enacted by the children, and specifically devised to celebrate 'differences', was entitled 'Kingdom of White'. It told the tale of a princess who was bored by her all-white kingdom. She was taken away by a kind fairy to witness places with a variety and range of different colours. One of the teachers created a song entitled 'Berbeda itu indah' ('Differences are beautiful') for the finale:

Verse 1

Differences are beautiful

Differences are beautiful

Differences are beautiful

Colourful is beautiful

You are red,

I am yellow

You are blue,

I am green

We don't need to be similar

Verse 2

Colourful is beautiful

You are thick, I am thin

You are tall,

I am short

Your hair is straight,

Mine is curly

We don't need to be similar.

The roles of the princess and the fairy were performed by Nadya and Husna, whilst the other girls took on the roles of flowers and birds, with the boys performing the roles of fishes.

Vina Adriany noted that, as she heard the words of the song, her thoughts prompted questions: 'What do we do with differences? Are all differences acceptable? If not, which ones are not?' These questions became important because the school obviously expected the children to perform traditional gender roles. Whilst the school encouraged a respect for differences it was also perpetuating sameness. Whilst the school appeared to value the 'children's attempt to become themselves', when it came to gender behaviour, the school required children's identity to be fixed and singular. The concept of differences did not seem to include gender with the result that traditional gender discourses were uncontested, and gender power relations remained unchallenged.

Critical question

How could the enactment of this story and its central song be adapted to include a gender dimension? How could this be done in a way that would not essentialise gender differences?

This story illuminates a lack of gender awareness which is repressed, interestingly, through the very emphasis on diversity that could potentially serve to increase a sensitivity to gender. For example, if the same classroom practice was changed to include a gender dimension the children's song might include the additional lines 'I'm a boy/You're a girl'. Yet this addition would just serve to illustrate that not only is there a gender blindness inbuilt into the song but also an essentialism about differences. If the story were to be re-written from a **feminist poststructuralist**/queer approach, the protagonist (who could perhaps be a gender-non-conforming person) would make the discovery that colours can be creatively mixed to form new colours.

Application of intersectionality to curriculum policy on diversity

The story provokes thought about how an intersectional approach to diversity can be put into practice and policy. **Intersectionality** (discussed in Chapter 1) is an ambitious theory when it comes to the application of the theory to policy and practice. How far is it really possible to devise policy and **pedagogy** that is based on an awareness and recognition of crosscutting social categories? The advantages of intersectionality as an analytic tool for devising policy is that it gives people more insight into the complexities of the world and of themselves (Hill Collins & Bilge, 2020). Yet this advantage is at the same time its disadvantage in so far as it creates an almost overwhelming complexity. Users of the theory try to consider the interdependent cross-cutting influences of a wide range of different social categories axes such as race, gender, class, disability, rather than a traditional single axis such as gender. This has led to the 'et cetera' problem identified by Cho et al. (2013).

> As intersectionality has traveled, questions have been raised regarding a number of issues ... the eponymous 'et cetera' problem – that is the number of categories and kinds of subjects (e.g. privileged, subordinate?) stipulated or implied by an intersectional approach. (p. 787)

The policy statements discussed above within the various national curricula demonstrate the 'et cetera' problem in exactly this way. I have noted two curriculum statements (Australian, Irish) that use lists of difference axes to guide educators to the differences that must be attended to using the catch-all 'et cetera'. One example is the Irish National Quality Framework for Early Childhood Education (Síolta: The National Quality Framework for Early Childhood Education, 2022), where guidance requests the avoidance of 'the depiction of stereotypical role models and cultural images (e.g. gender, culture, age, ability **etc**)' and the need to avoid 'bias (e.g. gender, colour, race, religious affiliation, family structure, socio economic status **et cetera**) within activities' (pp. 97–100).

However, what we might call 'single axis' concerns, such as my own focus on gender here in this book, continue to have an important place. Intersectional approaches do not pit one category of social inequality against another but recognise their interdependency. We may often have to emphasise or even overemphasise the importance of one key social category in order to compensate for its relative invisibility. In my case the category of gender has been a longstanding interest and growing area of research expertise, so it is my prime focus but increasingly I try to be aware of the ways it intersects other key axes of difference.

So, to conclude this section about gender's centrality on the curriculum I venture that it seems possible to have 'the best of both worlds'. It is possible, and desirable, to have a solid overall statement in curriculum guidance about the value of diversity but to elaborate on this with specific statements that detail pedagogical plans focusing on some of these categories discretely. The promotion of a gender-flexible pedagogy fits within this frame but requires specificity and status with national curricula in order to prevent gender blindness which leads to gender inequalities and the perpetuation of gender stereotypes.

How Does Gender Mediate New Curricular Values?

In the section which introduced this chapter, I discussed how a **curriculum**, or learning plan, for any age group is likely to reflect the values of those with the power to influence it. Assumptions about 'powerful knowledge', what counts as knowledge in society, are usually presented as fixed and taken for granted. However, when we look back at historical curriculum creation we can see how curricula change with the times, reflecting changes in the kinds of knowledge that are valued. Changes in society constantly demand new knowledge and skills and require the continuous development of our educational system, a point made in the overview of early childhood education curriculum development by Colwell (2015): 'as time has passed the content of the curriculum has altered' (p. 201).

It is interesting to spot how the curriculum is changing in ECE at the present time. One newer area of ECE activity that is worth mentioning is outdoor education. There is no doubt that there has been a huge surge of interest in outdoor education in ECE, shown in an expansion of outdoor educational spaces and in specialist outdoor focused schools such as forest schools, and beach schools. There is an emerging consensus that outdoor learning and play are good for young children's well-being and learning (Malone & Waite, 2016; Sando, 2019) and that schools and Early Years setting should be doing more to optimise children's connection to nature (Gill, 2014). How, if at all, is gender woven into this? What potential is there for a gender flexible pedagogy within it?

One relevant aspect is that there appears to be a correlation between the presence of male practitioners in ECE and the prevalence of outdoor education (Emilsen & Koch, 2010; Peeters et al., 2015). This is a somewhat problematic relationship because it can imply a traditional gendered division of labour for practitioners with the potential problem that men take over the outdoors forms of learning whilst women are allocated to the indoors work. However, a more nuanced conclusion is necessary in order to recognise the potential for an opening-up of curricular opportunities together with the expansion of different kinds of care and learning for young children. In Warin (2018), I argued that the greater presence of male teachers in ECE might help the ECE sector to broaden out its curriculum and identified outdoor education as an example.

A strong value for outdoor education and its close cousin 'place-based learning' is at the heart of an innovative project I have recently had the good fortune to evaluate. This ongoing project, located in the Morecambe Bay community in the North West of England, has brought various early childhood settings together in a storytelling strategy focused on a character called Eden Bear and known locally as the 'Eden Bear project'. My research aim was to examine how the outdoor and place-based elements of the project were working. I did not have an explicit aim to examine gender issues within this particular research project.

Case study

'Gender blindness' in the Eden Bear project

The Eden Bear Project is a small but vital cog in the ambitious new educational wheel identified as the Morecambe Bay Curriculum (MBC) representing the educational strand of Eden Project North (EPN) which is scheduled to be created very soon in the Morecambe Bay area. The MBC is an innovative, place-based, strategic reform and educational vision which integrates nature, education, health, community and the economy across the Bay. The Eden Bear Project has been devised by Early Years and Primary school educators, collectively for the EYFS who are working with the very young, the generation of children who are at the heart of the MBC which is focused on their future well-being. A character, a teddy bear named Eden Bear (EB), was chosen by EYFS leaders as a catalyst for prompting children's storytelling about place, and about life in Morecambe. The project's initiators chose a teddy bear because it has an iconic status as a friendly, non-threatening figure in fiction for children. A two-person research team led by myself set out to research the initial impacts of the project.

In our interviews with the project's creators, we quickly established that the bear was understood as a gender non-specific character. When we interviewed project leaders and participants, they emphasised the gender non-specific nature of the bear. Staff were committed to this aspect of EB, recognised the teaching potential concerning gender non-specificity and dedicated themselves to a careful use of gender-neutral language. For example one practitioner explained why the bear was a good device compared with a doll: 'Doll route too gender specific... **gender fluidity** important and high profile'. Some staff showed awareness of gender neutral language and attempted to use the pronoun 'they' or most often they referred to this character as 'the bear...'. Yet despite these mani-festations of **gender sensitivity** and interest from staff it was very common to spot how frequently the pronoun 'he' was adopted in describing EB's visits and impacts on the children. For example, one of many such instances was a teacher describing the value of the project 'part of EB'S success was groundwork done before *he* came and after *he* left'. The data include many such examples.

As a researcher involved in this project, I also found the use of the gender neutral pronoun to be challenging (see discussion by Tobia, 2016) and was aware of deliberately choosing synonyms for 'he' or 'she' opting for a phrase such 'this character', 'our new friend', 'Eden Bear', 'EB' or 'the visitor to Morecambe Bay'. However, I noticed that I sometimes reverted to 'he' with the same slippage illustrated above in the teachers' comments. Clearly the commitment to EB's gender non-specificity created a wonderful opportunity for a focus on the use of the gender-neutral pronoun. Yet this was not the specific focus of the project and indeed it was not my own focus within the evaluation. I could not give myself full marks for gender sensitivity on this occasion.

Critical question

Can you think of any times when you have been gender blind and missed an opportunity for creating a teachable moment that would expand ideas about gender?

The story above shows us that a **gender sensitivity** should underline all activities, practiced by Early Years practitioners who have developed gender-sensitive antennae. The lack of a continuing attention to gender, and the distraction of different foci in this project, made for an element of gender insensitivity. It reminds us that the educational goal of developing gender-sensitive children through the gender-sensitivities of their teachers is not a goal that can be simply plopped into the curriculum as a topic. As the **Fawcett Society** point out in their report 'Unlimited Potential' (2020), 'challenging gender stereotypes across the whole curriculum needs to be an explicit objective' (p. 26). Gender sensitivity is an *awareness*, a sensibility, that an early childhood educator (or early childhood researcher) should carry around with them so they are alert to opportunities to challenge gender stereotypes. The term 'gender flexible pedagogy' makes this point. It is about how gender sensitivity can potentially mediate the teaching and learning environment and form an underlying principle within teaching relationships.

Conclusions

This chapter has asked what the concept of curriculum means and how relevant it is to the concept of a gender-flexible pedagogy? The chapter arrives at five linked conclusions:

- Curriculum, a learning plan, is influenced by government views about knowledge and government priorities in setting out educational goals including for the very young.
- There is an insufficient attention given to gender in the ECE curriculum guidance of most countries although there are some notable exceptions that can provide positive models to emulate.

- Gender may feature in curricula as part of an 'et cetera' list of foci within broader expressions of values for diversity and equality. Whilst this intersectional approach has advantages, it can make gender invisible. We are far more likely to develop gender sensitivity, gender-sensitive antennae, if there is something specific about it on the curriculum for the Early Years – in guidance documents about what should be taught.
- As curricula change, it is important for gender issues to become embedded.

A gender-flexible pedagogy requires that gender is clearly and visibly part of the Early Years' menu.

REFLECTIVE QUESTIONS

- How far is it necessary to have an explicit gender focus written into the curriculum in order for Early Years practitioners and wider society to take it seriously?
- Is it better to have gender-focused goals within a broader agenda for equality, diversity and inclusion?

READER CHALLENGE

Phrase your ideal, gender-focused, curriculum goal for the 3–6-year-old age group.

3

Resources and Activities for Smashing Stereotypes

Introduction

The aim of this chapter is to continue the discussion about the 'what' of an Early Childhood Education **(ECE) gender-flexible pedagogy** now turning our attention to the things that young children do, and play with. We need to think about how far we, as educators, can manage resources and activities to smash **gender stereotypes** and create a set of gender-flexible experiences which will not trap children into gendered pathways. This chapter incorporates strategies about the provision of resources: toys, books and practical ideas for creating a gender-sensitive environment. It also discusses strategies for the management of resources, for example focusing on the significant barriers that can prevent ECE practitioners from challenging gender stereotypes.

The chapter is divided into two broad sections. The first aims to describe recent activity from campaigning groups in the United Kingdom who share the aim of challenging gender stereotypes and who, between them, have produced an inspiring array of ideas and resources for practitioners to use directly in primary schools and

ECE settings. This is structured by an overview of different types of resources: books; toys; activities; and the overall ECE environment. There is plenty here for practitioners to follow up such as lists of gender-challenging books for young children, and practical advice. I will also consider that most precious and potentially flexible resource – ourselves as teachers.

The second section then discusses the rather more subtle business of managing these resources and focuses on the obstacles that lie in the path of even the most gender-sensitive teachers. The chapter then presents two case studies of practices, one from Norway and one from Sweden. These have been aimed at enabling children to expand their learning experiences and demonstrate models of ingenious ways to prevent children getting confined into narrow gendered expectations based on traditional boy/girl toys and activities. They are discussed critically, unpacking their advantages and disadvantages. By the end of the chapter Early Years practitioners and researchers will have become aware of what resources are out there – and also how to make use of them. I conclude that ECE staff can only attempt to nip gender stereotyping in the bud through an ongoing and opportunistic use of resources.

The Provision of Stereotype Smashing Resources

In recent times there has been an explosion of interest in creating good resources to challenge stereotypes. In the United Kingdom, there has been a rise of campaigning groups who are all in various ways aiming to smash stereotypes inside and outside of education: **Lifting Limits**; **Smashing Stereotypes**; **Stonewall**; **Let Toys be Toys**, **Let Books Be Books**; **Let Clothes Be Clothes**; the **Fawcett Society**, the **NEU; Gender Action** (see References for websites). Throughout this book I refer to the vital contribution they are making, but in this chapter in particular I mention their work on the provision of resources and their strategies for raising gender awareness.

Toys

I begin with the all-important topic of doll play. This type of play is incredibly important for both boys and girls as it encourages social skills especially the potential to develop empathy (Hashmi et al., 2020). It gives children the opportunity to imagine the feelings and needs of their dolls. Doll play must be strategically inclusive to enable all children to engage in developing this skill. Staff need to create opportunities for doll play and provide a range of dolls representing the diversity of the wider world.

However, it is also worth pointing out that young children, especially the very young (two and three year olds), often turn non-figurative objects into people. Many observations of young children's play have shown me that the content of the play comes from the interaction of several different kinds of triggers or provocations

– the actual toy or object being only one. When the young child is motivated to undertake a nurturing activity, for whatever reason (such as mood, emotion, recent events), they can quickly turn any old object into a baby requiring food. For example young children will play parenting activities with a Daddy train and baby train. Similarly, dolls can be used to prompt a toy fight or for entirely unpredictable purposes. When I gave my 2-year-old a doll to play with, it was turned upside down and used for digging in the sand. This did not bode well for the nurturing approach I'd hoped to encourage towards the arrival of a new baby sibling! Indeed, there is a view that the very best kinds of toys for young children are those that are wide open to a whole range of different interpretations and uses and that therefore, by implication, avoid gender coding. Montessori schools adopt this approach very explicitly. Whilst Montessori toys are most famous for being made out of natural materials rather than plastics they are also designed to be simple and uncluttered so they can be used expansively through the child's imagination (MontiKids.com). As we know from decades of Vygotskian influenced research (Bennet et al., 1997; Jones & Reynolds, 1992; Wood & Attfield, 2013), ECE practitioners can creatively steer young children's play by providing the right kinds of open-coded material objects and through their own creative engagement in play. This may be especially important to enable both boys and girls to develop empathy, relationality and the basis for emotional literacy.

'Let Toys Be Toys' (LTBT) (2021) has developed resources for ECE practitioners exploring the attributes of different kinds of toys, how they help to support the **EYFS** and why it's vital that boys and girls are encouraged to take part in all kinds of play. They list toys/resources under the following categories: Outside, Home Corner, Role Play and Dressing Up, Jigsaws and Puzzles, Construction, and Small world in a gender-neutral language showing the advantages of the resources for the designated EYFS areas of learning. They also have a list of '8 ways to challenge stereotypes in EY settings', counteracting what Day (2020) (LTBT volunteer) terms the 'drip, drip, drip of gendered messaging, telling children that boys and girls can't like, or do the same things' (pp. 95–96). The LTBT campaign commenced in 2012 in the run-up to Christmas when a group of parents were disturbed by the heavy-handed use of gender stereotypes to sell toys and especially the use of gendered signs in toy shops with specific aisles separated for boys and girls. By the following Christmas '15 major UK retailers, … had agreed to take the signs down and let toys be toys' (Let Toys Be Toys', 2021). In 2016, the group's survey found 'no 'boys' or 'girls' signs in stores, and a 70% drop in gender labels and navigation on websites'. The organisation also examined TV advertisements (Let Toys Be Toys, 2015). They reveal a very clear pattern of advertisers exploiting gender stereotypes for marketing. They found that not one advertisement depicted a boy with baby or fashion dolls whilst only one of 25 adverts for toy vehicles included a girl. Boys were shown as active and aggressive with the advertising text emphasising power and conflict. Girls were depicted as passive, unless dancing, with the text based on fantasy, beauty and relationships (Let Toys Be Toys, 2021).

I interviewed Olivia Dickinson, a key member of Let Toys Be Toys since 2014, and our conversation explored why gender stereotypes are still so pervasive in society and difficult to challenge in educational settings.

Case study

Interview with Olivia Dickinson (Let Toys Be Toys)

Jo: What stops early childhood educators from tackling gender stereotypes?

Olivia: Often it's to do with what parents are saying. We get lots of anecdotes that children only get that sort of gender policing and encounter stereotypes when they start in a formal setting. That could be a nursery or a school. If it's a good nursery, practitioners are often able to challenge that straight away and they can challenge at the child's level. It's when, and I'm sure you've heard this, the parents make a fuss, 'Why are you letting my boy dress up?' In that sense the practitioners need the confidence and they need the understanding of why it matters. Some of the nurseries I've been in, they totally get it. But when there are young or only recently qualified staff, it's harder to make it clear. What we've talked about quite a lot [at LTBT] is the age of teachers and practitioners sometimes because what we've realised is that a lot of us in the campaign grew up in the seventies and eighties and to us there wasn't really gendered marketing. We avoided it mainly. We [at LTBT] realised that people in their twenties now think it's normal. So it started in the nineties. If they grew up with it, they can't always, it's that subconscious thing – they can't understand why it's a problem. Obviously some people have been really frustrated by it and that's why they've become teachers [Olivia then discusses a talk she gave to a young group of mainly female BEd students aged 19/20]. I found there were about two who got it straight away and were bothered by it and said they'd felt constrained as little girls. And the rest, I heard them say 'Well It doesn't really matter' and I even heard them say, and we talked about men ending up being senior leadership, and I heard them say 'Well it's just what men do'. And these are the people who are teaching our children! They don't get training about gender stereotypes and why it matters. I can see they haven't really thought about these things at all. They just haven't had to.

Jo: That's a very interesting answer – the fact that they just haven't thought about it. Because we get stuck in our own bubble about the things we are campaigning about, that matter to us, whilst younger people may have just become so used to a more strongly gendered world especially when it comes to advertising that they take it for granted.

Critical question

Olivia refers to how in the 1990s there was an increase within the toy industry of gendered marketing. Her thinking has been informed by the work of Elizabeth Sweet who argued (2015) that toys are more gendered than ever before. Olivia discusses how this may have affected the attitudes of different generations of teachers and Early Years practitioners. From your own experience, whether as a child or a parent, how do you think marketing of toys has changed in the last 30 years? How has this affected your own attitudes? (Your answer may perhaps depend on your own age as Olivia points out.)

Books, songs and media

Despite the rise in other forms of media in use within Early Years settings and children's homes, story books still have an impact – as the Fawcett Society report claims (Fawcett, 2020). The authors cite a study by Abad and Pruden (2013) which found that exposure to stereotype-smashing storybooks 'can lead to increasing play with counter-stereotypical toys, changing children's perceptions of what activities and jobs are appropriate for women and men, and widening children's aspirations' (p. 16).

The organisation 'Lifting Limits' has surveyed children's picture books and presents findings about the prevalence of sexism. It claims that:

> A review of the top 100 children's picture books published in 2018 found a child is 1.6 times more likely to read a picture book with a male rather than female lead, and seven times more likely to read a story that has a male villain in it than a female baddie. Male characters outnumbered female characters in more than half of the books, while females outnumber males less than a fifth of the time. (Lifting Limits, 2021)

This organisation also examined which famous figures are explicitly studied within the primary school **curriculum**, examining the portrayal of inventors (12 men, no woman), explorers (5 men, no woman), artists (8 men, 1 woman) and musical composers (8 men, 1 woman) (Lifting Limits, 2021). The ECE practitioners need to be aware of the subtle and not-so-subtle messages that young children receive from the cumulative impact of this gender blind selection.

In order to raise awareness, an ECE setting, or group of settings, can undertake their own book audit following the advice of Price (2018) and the example of Lifting Limits. A simple counting of female versus male protagonists can be thought-provoking, especially if discussed in a whole-staff group. It is also very illuminating to search for, and discuss, portrayals of gender non-conformity. Subsequent choices about replenishing the library can then be made to ensure a much better representation of gender roles using suppliers like 'Letterbox Library' who analyse each book that they sell for diversity criteria, and also the organisation 'We Need Diverse Books'.

A focus on children's literature was the initial focus of the United Kingdom's National Education Union (NEU) project 'Breaking the Mould' (Jennett, 2018). It harnessed a detailed study of five primary schools who were given training to consider how to challenge gender stereotypes in nursery and primary school. The project team decided to help school staff begin their research by providing them with a range of children's books, which challenge gender stereotypes. In the course of the project, staff found other titles and introduced colleagues to their favourites. Similar work has also been undertaken by the organisation Stonewall who campaign for LGBTQ+ inclusivity. I have combined the book list from the NEU report (Jennett, 2018) with the booklists from Stonewall that challenge gender stereotypes for the 2–4 age group and the 5–7 age group. The overall list is presented below.

Book list for challenging gender stereotypes

Baking with Dad (Aurora Cacciapuoti, published by Child's Play, ISBN 1846437547)

Jacob's New Dress (Sarah Hoffman and Ian Hoffman, published by Albert Whitman & Company, ISBN 0807563730)

Julián is a Mermaid (Jessica Love, published by Candlewick, ISBN 9780763690458)

Super Duper You (Sophie Henn, published by Puffin, ISBN 0141385480)

Tough Chicks (Cece Meng, published by Clarion Books, ISBN 0618824154)

Tough Guys Have Feelings Too (Keith Negley)

Jump (Michelle Magorian, published by Walker Books Ltd, ISBN 0744589614)

Oliver Button Is a Sissy (Tomie dePaola, published by HMH Books for Young Readers, ISBN 0156681404)

10,000 Dresses (Marcus Ewert - ISBN 978-1583228500)

Amazing Grace (Mary Hoffman - ISBN 978-1845077495)

Bill's New Frock (Anne Fine - ISBN 978-1405233187)

The Boy in A Dress (David Walliams - ISBN 978-0007279036)

The Boy with Pink Hair (Perez Hilton - ISBN 978-0451234209)

The Different Dragon (Jennifer Bryan - ISBN 978-0967446868)

Dogs Don't Do Ballet (Anna Kemp - ISBN 978-1847384744)

Girls Are Best (Sandi Toksvig - ISBN 978-1862304291)

It's a George Thing! (David Bedford - ISBN 978-1405228053)

Man's Work! (Annie Kubler - ISBN 978-0859535878)

The Odd Egg (Emily Gravett - ISBN 978-0230531352) T

The Paperbag Princess (Robert Munsch - ISBN 978-0920236161)

Piggybook (Anthony Browne – ISBN 978-1406313284)

Pirate Girl & The Princess Knight (Cornelia Funke, available in *A Princess, A Knight and One Wild Brother*, ISBN 978-0545042413)

Princess Pigsty (Cornelia Funke – ISBN 978-1905294329)

Red Rockets and Rainbow Jelly (Sue Heap – ISBN 978-0140567854)

The Sissy Duckling (Harvey Fierstein – ISBN 978-1416903130)

Super Daisy (Kes Gray – ISBN 978-1862309647)

The Turbulent Term of Tyke Tiler (Gene Kemp – ISBN 978-0571230945)

It is fun and very revealing to swap round sex pronouns in children's books. Many creative and gender-sensitive practitioners enjoy making a deliberate reversal of gender roles in stories. The same also applies to songs and nursery rhymes. Given that some practitioners engage in this gender-flexible type of practice I was particularly disappointed by an incidence of gender blind practice I witnessed during my ethnographic study at **Acorns** where such opportunities had not been taken (Warin, 2018). Practitioners were leading the children in a rendition of the ubiquitous song 'The Wheels on the Bus go Round and Round'. There are so very many versions of this song now and it lends itself well to the changing and addition of new verses. Consequently, there seems to be no excuse to come across traditional gender stereotypes such as 'The women on the bus go chatter chatter', which is what I heard on that day. Interestingly the Fawcett Society's report on gender stereotypes found that in three video versions of this nursery rhyme the bus drivers were male.

There has been a strong research tradition on feminist engagement with children's traditional stories and Fairy Tales exposing how fairy tales 'perpetuate the patriarchal status quo by making female subordination seem romantically desirable and an inescapable fate' (Rowe, 2010, p. 237). A key early influence was Bronwyn Davies who supported children to invert gender roles in traditional stories and break out of gender stereotypes (Davies, 2003). Feminist retellings turn the traditional roles 'upside down' (Westland, 2006), for example in the Norwegian study of a retelling of the Princess and the Pea (Meland, 2020).

There has been some important research on examining how children actually respond to the inversion of roles in children's songs and stories ever since Davies (2003) discovered a gap between the good intentions of the authors and the ways that children were actually hearing the stories. Bartholmaeus (2015) followed up this finding and investigated 6/7-year-old Australian children's responses to four feminist picture books (Cinder Edna, Piggybook, William's Doll, A Fire Engine for Ruthie). She found that 'children had difficulty in understanding these stories in the context of the dominant gender discourse they were familiar with' (p. 939). She concludes that teachers need to ensure that there are supportive activities around the use of such resources such as class discussions and related activities. Wee et al. (2017) used a critical literacy approach to investigate 5-year-old Korean children's responses to fairy/folk tales. The work took place over a whole series of critical literacy sessions – enabling children's gradual development of a criticality of traditional gender stereotypes. This is a particularly interesting study because it demonstrates a recognition that children's understandings about gender stereotypes, and their ability to challenge and critique stereotypes, requires an ongoing and persistent attention and is also a challenge to critics who argue that 5-year-olds are too young to develop this capacity.

The organisation 'Let Books be Books', an offshoot of 'Let Toys be Toys', was launched on World Book Day in 2014 in conjunction with Letterbox library, to persuade publishers of children's books to stop labelling and promoting books 'for boys' or 'for girls' ('Let Books be Books', 2021). The campaign was applauded by various influential journalists who gave it press coverage in the United Kingdom and was also supported by some high-profile children's authors and poets. The children's publisher Usborne announced it would not be commissioning any new boys/girls' titles, a strategy that was then picked up and followed by many of the most respected children's publishing houses and even by a well-known stationery outlet which ceased to supply gendered activity books.

The provision of excellent resources can only take us so far in trying to prevent gender stereotyping. Later in this book (Chapter 7), there will be discussion about one of the most important resources of all in challenging children's gender stereotypes – the use of ourselves, teachers, as resources. In addition, it is necessary to develop strategies for **managing** these resources and making sure they get used and get used effectively.

The Management of Stereotype-Smashing Resources

In addressing this challenge, it is worth considering the barriers that face practitioners in harnessing good resources to challenge stereotypes. So the chapter now moves on to examine what these barriers are. I discuss: a fear about what parents will say; a worry that children will become 'confused'; a concern that such strategies are too controlling, preventing children's free choice and stopping them from becoming 'themselves'.

A fear about what parents will say

Early Years practitioners may feel constrained in their willingness to challenge gender stereotypes by worries about how some parents might react. However, there is growing evidence that most parents are strongly supportive of this aim and indeed many parents feel that schools should be making a point of challenging stereotypes so that parents and schools can join forces to counteract the strong gender differentiation that is so rife within the wider society (Fawcett, 2020; Let Toys Be Toys, 2021). Yet we know that certain groups of parents are resistant and have a strong family culture of gender differences especially where this is influenced by religious beliefs. For example, in my joint research with Vina Adriany in Indonesia we had to take account of the religious beliefs upheld in many Moslem families that gender differences are 'essential' to each individual, deeply innate within the person, God-given, and part of their essential nature or 'kodrat' (Warin & Adriany, 2017). Practitioners need to work especially sensitively with parents who have culturally informed resistances to challenging gender stereotypes. This will be discussed later in the book in Chapter 6.

One of the most frequently voiced fears that occupy practitioners is that parents are concerned about their children being bullied if they do not conform to gender expectations and this seems to be particularly so for parents of boys. They have some grounds for this fear since the Fawcett Society report on their poll for evidence on gender stereotyping that:

> Parents, particularly parents of boys, are worried about bullying due to gender non-conformity. 61% said they would worry about bullying if their son behaved differently to what is seen as 'normal' for their gender, compared to 47% in relation to their daughter. (Fawcett, 2020, p. 19)

Young children police each other's gender conformity, and non-conformity. Even young children are familiar with and make use of homophobic language as Jones pointed out in his impassioned plea, on the 50th anniversary of the partial decriminalisation of homosexuality in England and Wales:

> Society is diseased with homophobia and transphobia… used to police and enforce gender norms… internalised by children at the earliest age. Gay, queer, poof: these words are flung at boys – straight or queer – for any behaviour deemed 'unmanly', from a lack of athletic prowess, not getting into enough fights. (Jones, 2017)

Whilst there have been many strides towards the rights and inclusion of LGBT+ people including the all-important recognition of same sex marriage in 2013, nevertheless, there are alarming statistics that confirm that homophobia is still pervasive. The campaigning group Stonewall uses the current strapline: 'Our work is not finished' and their site contains evidence of the prevalence and outcomes of homophobic bullying (Stonewall, 2021). The report from NEU (Jennett, 2018) cites parents who have been concerned about their children, especially sons being bullied in school and labelled 'gay' if they break out of gender norms for example displaying a love of kittens or having the colour pink on their clothing (two examples mentioned in this report). Homophobia and a fear of homophobic bullying exerts a huge and often invisible influence on a resistance to challenging gender stereotypes.

A worry that children are too young to understand and will become 'confused'

Sometimes critics of a stereotype-smashing agenda will say that children are too young to understand the concept of stereotypes and that they could become confused by attempts to develop their questioning of, and criticality towards them. There are two interwoven discourses here. One is based in developmental psychology and acknowledges that young children are in the business of inventing simple categorisations of their worlds which can actually indeed be understood as stereotypes. The other is about children's innocence and a need to protect them from 'adult' concepts.

Cognitive psychologists, linguists and others tell us that a child makes sense of their world by developing cognitive categories or schema and that these become more differentiated as the child develops (Bornstein & Arteberry, 2010). For example a very young child, a toddler, might use the word 'Dog' for any animal that they see and will then gradually begin to learn new words to differentiate different kinds of animals. In the same way, young children are continuously picking up on clues to help them differentiate males from females with some well-researched clues such as their use of key gender markers like hair length, colours and clothing (MacNaughton, 2000). Of course, these gender signifiers are all social constructions of gender deeply embedded in our society. Should we not perhaps be helping young children to develop and sustain simple homogenous categories relating to a clear binary distinction between males and females, between boy stuff and girl stuff? Is it confusing for young children to have these categories 'troubled'? Clearly, the reader will understand, this is a Devil's Advocate question. My answer is that 'confusion' is absolutely necessary for learning at any age – for developing increasingly differentiated and less homogenous categories. For example, following up the animal example above, the young child gradually learns to differentiate between lots of different kinds of animals after making the initial binary distinction between animal and non-animal. Many young children often find 'upside down' worlds are humorous precisely because such counter examples break the categorisation 'rules'. They may be amused, not confused, as they expand their learning.

Some of the most thoughtful work undertaken in recent times by gender-focused campaigning groups suggest strategies for teachers that rely simply on a teacher questioning a child at exactly the right moment. For example a teacher might make the most of those occasions when a child makes a strong claim about a rigid gender rule ('Only boys do that', 'That's just for girls') following the NEU advice to question gender stereotypes whenever they appear (Jennett, 2018, p. 7). Better still, ECE teachers can break gender rules themselves as deliberate way of confounding simplistic **gender binary** rules. A male ECE teacher, for example, has much potential power to smash stereotypes by provoking and then making the most of gender rule-breaking, creating teachable moments about gender stereotypes. This might be though a simple choice based on physical appearance such as wearing nail varnish and then, most importantly, ensuring that this behaviour gets noticed and discussed. In line with this advice, the NEU report (Jennett, 2018) makes the following point for teachers who want to address gender stereotyping:

> Remember to inspire as well – and to not be afraid to surprise and even confuse children with new ideas. It is often through confusion that our minds open up to new possibilities. (Jennett, 2018, p. 27)

The discourse of children's innocence and a concern that they need protecting from 'adult knowledge' has been well noted in ECE research. Traditionally, childhood has been presented as a period of innocence from the seventeenth century onwards (Robinson, 2013) constructed as a time to be protected from difficult and controversial 'adult' concerns (Blaise, 2005; Kehilly, 2002; Renold, 2005). This protective approach creates a taboo around topics of sexuality. However, Early Childhood Educators are in an ideal position to disrupt gender normalising discourses in their pedagogies and practices (Robinson & Diaz, 2006; Warin & Price, 2020). A sympathetic and encouraging adult response to gender non-conformity is very likely to benefit all children because it goes some way towards removing the pernicious influence of a rigid gender binary and accentuates the accessibility of difference. A nice example occurred when a group of Swedish ECE researchers played me a video of children's play about rituals including wedding play. They were delighted during our joint viewing of a particular incident, which they translated for me, when one child corrected another who said that women could only marry men. The ECE practitioners in the videoed classroom picked up on this and affirmed the child's challenge.

A worry that such strategies are too controlling

The Swedish video described above is noteworthy because it was a child rather than an ECE practitioner who raised the topic of same-sex weddings resisting the norm of the heterosexual wedding. Such comments, offered by children themselves, are invaluable to the gender-sensitive teacher. They are especially valuable because they make the most of the child's own agency and alleviate another concern that is often levelled at those who try to engage young children in stereotype-smashing: that such teacher behaviour is too 'controlling', insufficiently child-centred, operationalising the teacher's agenda and not the child's. Adriany and Warin's critique of child-centredness (2014) shows how this shibboleth of ECE can actually work to perpetuate a gender blind approach.

Limiting or unlimiting? Case studies of practice in Norway and Sweden

I am aware of a contradiction, a paradox, with regard to teachers' management of gender-challenging resources for young children. It concerns the management of choice and how a deliberate strategy to constrain choice and limit children's play can actually work, in the longer term, as a strategy for freeing up potential, lifting gender limits. I can illustrate this by describing the practice I witnessed in a Norwegian pre-school during the **GenderEYE project**.

Case study

Limiting choice in Granåsen setting Norway

I visited Granåsen Early Childhood Education and Care (ECEC) setting on the outskirts of Trondheim, Norway, surrounded by forest and well known for its outdoor education focus as well as its high proportion of male staff with a 50:50 gender balanced staff team. Of several noteworthy practices, one in particular stood out with regard to challenging gender stereotypes. This was a gender strategic control of access to toys and play resources.

Picture a minimalist classroom with white walls and pale wood furniture such as versatile child-sized cubes which could be transformed equally well into a bus, cosy cushioned reading area, or home corner. When I view the room first thing in the morning it is supplied with dolls, doll-sized furniture and cookware. There is nothing else to play with in the room. Later in the day the same room has undergone a complete transformation whilst the children are out of doors. Now the room is entirely equipped with transport toys: train tracks, roads, cars, lorries, trains and buses.

In this way the children's choices are carefully limited and managed to ensure that all children are exposed to a wide range of resources.

Critical question

How far do you think this kind of practice goes against the important principle of responding to the personal preferences of 'the unique child'?

Let's discuss this practice in a little more detail and engage with it critically. In some ways it appears to work directly against the strong child-centredness of most Early Years settings, enshrined in the curriculum statements of most countries in statements about the 'unique child'. The practice described above appears to constrain children's choices, imposing rather than lifting limits, by reducing the range of toys that are available in the environment. However, this carefully managed practice ensures that children become familiar with a much wider range of toys over time and therefore it does indeed have a longer term impact of increasing rather than decreasing the range of resources they will engage with. It creates the potential for 'everybody can do everything', a phrase that represents an ideal expressed by staff in the NEU report on gender stereotypes (Jennett, 2018, p. 7).

Allowing young children to have 'free choice' may appear to be a child-centred aim but gendered habits can become entrenched quickly. The NEU study (Jennett, 2018) found that the staff noticed that children were more likely to gravitate to gender-conformist pursuits when they were left to their own devices (p. 7). It becomes harder to intervene in children's habituated behaviours and encourage them to change their choices as clear preferences set in. Pre-school staff work hard to note what children are interested in and what activities they seem to be drawn to. So a deliberate challenge to children's preferences feels like a violation of the crucial principle of the child's free choice. Practitioners often wonder how they can bring about a change in play habits and indeed whether they *should* bring about change as it might interfere with the child's overall comfort and well-being. The practice described in the Norwegian pre-school tries to nip this problem in the bud by preventing a strong habituation to certain choices.

In their comprehensive recent report, entitled 'Unlimited Potential', the Fawcett Society identify many commercial influences at play which entrench gender stereotypes. Interestingly they describe how children's engagement with media, especially the online content of YouTube videos, traps children into an ever narrowing choice of content. Video platforms can have a negative impact in terms of stereotyping because they use algorithms to determine which video will be shown next, based on similarity to the previous video. We can see how pernicious and constraining this marketing strategy is. However, interestingly, it may be that teachers of young children can sometimes operate, quite unwittingly, in a similar way. They may entrench children's preferences from the kind but misplaced aim to develop a consistency of preference in the child, believing this to support the development of the young child's sense of self and relatedly their self-esteem. For example, at **Acorns** nursery (Warin, 2018), a large wall chart identifies each child's interests so that all staff will be able to respond to that child knowing a little about their preferred activities. Staff here believe that children's preferences determine who they are and that when staff recognise the children's likings they can reinforce the child's developing sense of self. Of course this practice has many benefits in terms of the child's overall well-being and feeling of being 'known', recognised and affirmed. However, it also risks the reinforcement of habitual preferences, when these become strongly gendered then it is hard to break out of these patterns. The sensitive ECE practitioner finds a balance between their developing knowledge and affirmation of each child's personal preferences alongside opportunities for expansion of them.

In managing resources to garner children's unlimited potential and prevent limiting stereotypes, ECE practitioners also need to be aware of children's peer group preferences. Children's choices about activities and resources are usually influenced by their choices about the people in the room too. This subtle and crucial interaction between plaything preferences and playmate preferences is apparent in another practical gender-focused strategy that was undertaken in a Swedish pre-school described in the case study below.

Case study

Attempt to manage the resources in a Swedish preschool class (adapted from Lindahl & Hjalmarsson, 2016)

Gender researchers, Annica Löfdahl and Maria Hjalmarsson, report on their study of a Swedish pre-school. This ethnographic study, spread over 18 months, harnessed video recordings and observational field notes to explore the setting's aims to create a gender conscious environment, fulfilling the Swedish preschool curriculum which explicitly addresses equality between genders. They report on the gender conscious strategy planned by staff to ensure equal rights for boys and girls 'to explore and develop interest and skills without limitations set by stereotyped gender roles' and to create the possibility of gender-crossing.

   The staff decided to dismantle the home corner, where the girls were used to playing with dolls, stove, kitchen utensils, prams and traditional housework tools. Instead, they distributed these playthings throughout the nursery, for example placing the stove in the Lego area, and the prams in a couple of smaller rooms. However, the researchers noticed that, contrary to the staff intentions, this strategy seemed to intensify the children's own segregation of play on gender lines. The girls simply recreated the home corner in a different part of the pre-school gathering together materials for making a new home, hanging curtains and creating a new kitchen area where they could cook, take care of their dolls, do the laundry and hang the washing out to dry. The researchers describe an incident when a group described as 'rough boys' attacked the recreated home using tools such as plastic knives as weapons, tearing down the washing, stamping on it and upsetting the girls.

Critical question

How else could the pre-school staff have intervened to change the established, gendered pattern of play in this classroom where girls were strongly identified with home corner play?

This gender-conscious **pedagogy** failed in two ways. First, staff were not sufficiently aware of the different kinds of masculinities and femininities within the broad categories of boy and girl and how these were played out in children's peer group interactions. Second, they failed to engage the children's own voices in planning their strategy. The researchers also suggest that the gender consciousness motives of the staff denigrated the girls' wish to engage in caring roles. The case study shows the interaction of peer preferences and toy preferences. It also shows the need to take account of children's agency and listen to their views in planning such strategies. Sometimes young children's responses are unpredictable.

Conclusions

- It is important to familiarise and equip ourselves with some of the excellent resources that are available to import into Early Years settings.
- Gender-sensitive resources such as 'upside down' stories, and other gender stereotype reversal resources, should be managed as part of ongoing work with children. We have also seen examples in this chapter of specific long-term, focused, projects to develop gender awareness in a setting (the Korean study by Wee et al. the NEU project, reported in Jennett, 2018).
- With regard to the management of good-quality gender-bending resources the conclusion is that such resources need to be readily at hand to support the spontaneous discussions that arise as part of classroom interactions. Whereas with older children this might take the form of some explicit teaching on gender stereotypes, with younger children it is more a question of responding spontaneously 'in the moment'. In this way ECE teachers can harness and create teachable moments and build up a trajectory of discussions and related practices.
- Building up the young child's capacity to recognise and question gender stereotypes needs constant reinforcement especially as the developing child is simultaneously bombarded with the gender stereotypes that exist in child-focused marketing and in so much of children's culture.
- A detailed knowledge of individual children together with an understanding of peer group friendship patterns and class dynamics is necessary for a careful and targeted management of relevant resources.

As with the last chapter on curriculum, we come to the conclusion again that gender is not something that can simply be inserted into the activities of an ECE class or setting. However good the resources are for smashing stereotypes, they need skilful deployment by sensitive teachers and harnessed as part of an ongoing strategy for developing a gender-flexible pedagogy.

━━━━━ REFLECTIVE QUESTION ━━━━━

- How far should ECE teachers engineer children's opportunities to engage with a diversity of resources including those that are gender non-traditional?

━━━━━ READER CHALLENGE ━━━━━

Engage in doll play with one or more boys, showing them how to change a nappy. If you are working in an ECE setting or a pre-school, invite a father to demonstrate this with his own baby.

Section II

The 'Who' of Gender Flexible Pedagogy: Who Is Implicated in Delivering It?

4

A Diverse Workforce

Introduction

I now aim to unpack the term '**gender flexible pedagogy**' a little more in this chapter and the next one with regard to teachers and teaching. I commence with a consideration of the last, important part of that phrase: **pedagogy**. I discuss its meanings and uses and especially its relevance to Early Childhood Education (ECE) across the globe. I then consider policy on the diversification of the **ECE** workforce, focusing on recent English government policy and also the staffing policy of an outstanding Children's Centre. Here I refer again to the concept of **intersectionality** presented in chapter one revealing how key social categories have woven together to bring about the stagnation of a homogenous ECE workforce in England that is female and white. It is well recognised across the globe that gender is the key defining characteristic of the ECE workforce with an average male proportion of less than 3% (OECD, 2018; Warin et al., 2021). However, ethnic minorities are also under-represented in European countries (Tembo, 2020).

Why does the homogeneity of the workforce matters? Why do we need a diverse workforce? In answering these questions, the chapter moves on to a consideration of the value of adult role models in ECE. Then I turn from the more general focus on diversification of the workforce to consider the *gender*-diversification of the ECE sector. Here my focus is particularly on the extraordinarily low proportion of men employed in ECE, a phenomenon that has been the focus of my recent research. I discuss findings from the GenderEYE research project (Warin et al., 2020) where data were collected to identify characteristics of the male section of the workforce.

A training toolkit was also created for the recruitment and support of men. I draw from this to discuss why it is so important for the sector to have a clear rationale for increasing the presence of men in the workforce. I commence this section about *who* delivers a gender flexible pedagogy by revisiting the concept of pedagogy which was overviewed in Chapter 1 and is now discussed more fully.

Pedagogy

Pedagogy is often understood as a synonym for 'teaching' but it is so much more. It also signals the underlying aims, philosophies and the wider body of research and knowledge about teaching and has often been translated as 'the science of teaching' (Fielding & Moss, 2011). Simon (1981) wrote a provocative text entitled 'Why no pedagogy in England?' suggesting that teaching in England was led by pragmatism, a 'what works' approach, which was focused especially, in primary schools, on the mechanics of instilling the '3 Rs' (Reading Writing and Arithmetic). He compared this English pragmatism to a much more coherent and systematic approach to teaching on the continent. Fielding and Moss (2011) and Alexander (2004) also support the superiority of continental Europe regarding a deeper attitude to pedagogy: 'the continental view of pedagogy, especially in northern, central and eastern Europe, brings together within one concept the act of teaching and the body of knowledge, argument and evidence in which it is embedded' (Alexander, 2004, p. 10).

The concept of pedagogy is more able to flourish within ECE than in later stages of the education system where a stronger neoliberal influence on educational performance and outcomes creates a school culture of 'education-in-its-narrowest sense' (ENS). This is a term coined by the radical educators Fielding and Moss (2011) to contrast an education focused on purely cognitive capacities with their radical holistic philosophy based on 'education-in-its broadest-sense' (EBS) which they describe as:

> ... fostering and supporting the general well-being and development of children and young people, and their ability to interact effectively with their environment and to live a good life... with the goal that both the individual and the society flourish. (p. 46)

Fielding and Moss suggest that a rich tradition of European pedagogy, derived from social pedagogy, is the basis of their EBS vision. However, this broad educational philosophy has become 'lost in translation', narrowed and simplified in English educational usage. Social pedagogy emphasises: well-being (for both the individual and the wider society); holistic learning; relationship-centredness (seeing children as part of a group); empowerment of children through recognition of their rights.

The term 'pedagogy' is especially useful for my purposes in this book because the expansiveness of the concept makes it relevant for encapsulating a whole approach to challenging gender in what is taught, who teaches, and how. A pedagogy emphasises the relationality of teaching, encompassing the well-being and empowerment of children. It has the 'whole child' at its heart and values the child's development as a contributor to their wider community. Early childhood educators are often models, par excellence, of pedagogues delivering EBS, if only the rest of the education world would take note and learn.

Having considered the value of the concept of pedagogy, we now consider *who* is well positioned to deliver a gender flexible pedagogy. Who are the best people for this? What does the current ECE workforce look like? What can be done to diversify it? I consider this question initially by focusing on the English workforce and the quite recent workforce strategy recommendations made by the English **DfE** in 2017 (DfE, 2017b).

The diversification of the workforce

The main focus of the DfE's 2017 'Workforce Strategy for the Early Years' (DfE, 2017b) was the quality, specifically the qualifications, of staff in this sector. In the section headed 'Attracting staff to join the sector', the strategy identifies that one of five foci is 'Diversity of the workforce'. However, there is nothing about the *range* of missing social categories of difference and diversity within the workforce. For example, there is nothing about the whiteness or the age of the profession as whole. Instead, the document focused on the gender diversification of the sector, which was interpreted as the recruitment, support and retention of male staff. Whilst this was a very welcome focus to those, such as myself, who care deeply about developing a mixed gender workforce, it is a shortcoming that diversification was not interpreted more broadly. Perhaps the nearest the document gets to a statement about the overall 'diversity' of the workforce is the statement: 'We also need to attract people into the sector with enthusiasm and dedication to working with young children' (p. 4). The sub text here (and it is very buried) seems to be that Early Years managers should not only be concerned with levels of qualifications but should take a wider approach to finding practitioners with a diversity of interests, aptitudes, qualifications and skills and that, most importantly, they should be highly motivated to work with young children. The document was published soon after a hot debate had taken place about the necessity for ECE recruits to have gained specific levels in their Maths and English GCSEs (see Bonetti, 2018, p. 21). Some felt this was essential to raise the overall profile of the early years and develop a more highly qualified workforce. Others felt that too much emphasis on conventional academic school qualifications might exclude those with other qualities to offer the sector. Many ECE managers have now taken a 'values led approach to recruitment' (Warin et al., 2020) aiming to develop a diverse staff team with a wide range of capabilities who are able to respond creatively and flexibly to the range of needs and interests that young children present.

Intersectionality in Creating a Diverse Workforce

A values-led approach was evident in an outstanding children's centre in the North of England which I had the good fortune to visit as a researcher between 2014 and 2019. A highly visible feature of my visits to this centre was the varied workforce. The centre had an unusually high proportion of male teachers (the feature that led me there in the first place), but it also had a noticeable representation of different age groups amongst the staff. Most significantly, and unusually, I met with Asian and Eastern European practitioners in addition to white English practitioners from the North of England. The centre was a **Children's Centre** offering its own training routes for Early Years qualifications, following the lead of a handful of pioneering Children's Centres. (These were created in England from 2003 to reduce social inequalities through the provision of services for children and their families incorporating educational provision.) I recently held a conversation with the manager of this centre, to look back on her staffing strategy and her attempt to diversify her workforce.

— Case study —

Interview with Theresa Gilmour (pseudonym), Manager of Children's Centre in North England

JW: How did you manage to achieve the rich and varied workforce that was so visible on the occasions when I've visited your centre?

TG: Yeah. It was a deliberate thing but some of it was down to luck... When I took over the nursery school in 2003 – it was all women – all middle-aged women actually – predominantly white middle-aged women. It was a small school. A tiny building. Not many children. But the community we were serving was very diverse. We were then told that we were going to move into a new building and develop into a Children's Centre. So, we knew we had an opportunity to recruit lots of new staff. That gave us the opportunity to really think about and focus on the sort of people that we wanted. It was important that the parents could find people that they could relate to and that represented that community. Well, it was absolutely crucial. We thought about how we'd do this, and we were recruiting a lot of staff and we knew that through that normal recruitment (obviously always selecting the best people, there's no doubt about that, there was no compromise there) we'd have the opportunity to really get people into the building who would be reflective of the community, the wider community.

Alongside that – given that we were involved in various networks, various meetings with the local authority, other partners in the community – we met lots of people. So, if we were coming across somebody who we thought 'this person would be good', we actively encouraged them to apply for posts that we had available. The other thing was that we made a conscious decision – which a lot of organisations won't do – we took lots and lots of students and volunteers… That was a good way of getting people to come and spend some time to get to know us and see if this was a place they could work. And we decided then that we would start taking apprentices… we managed to recruit quite a lot of our staff through the apprenticeship route.

JW: How would you describe the diversity in terms of ethnicities, race.?

TG: We used to have a big board with everybody's photos and listed the languages they spoke. It was phenomenal really. We were amazed at the range of languages: Malaysian, Portuguese, Arabic, Slovakian, Latvian, Croatian, Serbian, Bosnian, Polish, Punjabi, Pashto, Spanish. It was an eye-opener at that point to think how many languages we had amongst the team. Interestingly though as well-sometimes the parents wouldn't automatically latch on to somebody who was like themselves. Sometimes they wanted somebody who was very different to them which was fine as well because that's what the diversity offers…We would try to allocate the key worker who spoke the language of the family … but sometimes the child would want somebody different because they had struck up a relationship [with another practitioner].

Critical question

Should managers in less varied communities only choose representatives of that particular community?

This manager exemplifies an approach that the whole sector could learn from. It is an excellent example of intersectionality for a practical purpose (although not termed as such by the key protagonists who executed this approach). In a similar vein, Tembo (2021, p. 71) has also pointed out that it is crucial to have a teaching force that represents society and points out that 'the **ECEC** profession remains overwhelmingly white'. He has undertaken research with black ECE workers to make their experiences visible and is critical of 'a colour-blind narrative that has led many people to think issues around race do not merit discussion in the ECE context, or that children do not "see" race' (p. 71). His critique echoes the comments I made in the previous chapter about the 'innocence' of children and assumptions about their capacity to handle complexity and differentiation. Tembo quotes from one of his teacher participants, Mandy, who recognised that Black parents welcomed her presence feeling '…thank God there is someone I could talk to that looks like me' (p. 77). He suggests that it is particularly valuable for black children who are very likely to benefit from seeing black adults in education as influential figures.

Intersectional research on the ECE workforce has been undertaken in the United States and is presented by Rohrrman et al. (2021) who draw attention to the high visibility of gender and race as dimensions of difference in the ECE workforce. Echoing the point made by Tembo's Mandy, these authors describe a push from some ECE managers, policy-makers and academics to undertake a proactive recruitment of a diversified workforce:

> Put simply, children from minority communities in general and Black and
> Latino males in particular are in dire need of seeing themselves reflected in
> the ECEC professionals with whom they spend much of their time as young
> children. (p. 36)

What is it like for an ECE practitioner who belongs to more than one of these
most visible minority staff groups? How do race and gender influence the everyday
lives of such people and influence their decision to remain in the profession? An
international collaborative book edited by Brody et al. (2021), *Exploring Career Trajectories of Men in the Early Childhood Education and Care Workforce*, examines men's
narratives about persisting in, and dropping out of, ECEC. South African researcher
Deevia Bhana contributes an account to this book about the experiences of Senzo, a
Black African teacher who commenced work in ECE and then left the profession.

──── **Case study** ──

Senzo's experience as a Black male early childhood education teacher (based on extracts from the book by Brody et al., 2021 and a chapter in this book by Bhana et al., 2021)

Senzo lives and works in South Africa and is aged 28.

'Black African, he grew up in poverty with a strong political leaning towards the
African National Congress, despising apartheid's injustices. As a university education
student, he occupied a key role in the student representative council. He enrolled for the
Bachelor of Education in Foundation Phase (FP) as there were bursaries teaching in the
early years. His strong sense of being a Zulu man and peer and family pressure to
perform masculinity drove him away from FP. He is currently teaching in high school, an
active member of the South African Democratic Teachers Union, and is happy with
working with teenagers' (Brody et al., 2021, p. 211).

Senzo's story about his career in ECE, as narrated to Bhana, demonstrates the
intersection of race and gender as important influences. He left the ECE sector even
though he had a specialist university degree for teaching in this sector. His story includes
his experience of his relationships with female colleagues who expressed the view that
they did not like male students. This was even more difficult because he was black. Bhana
et al. write about his perceptions regarding a lack of empathy from his colleagues. 'He
claimed that white men can't fully understand his challenges in the same way women
can't fully understand what men in ECEC have to handle: "Even if white males were there,
they would not have understood the pressure that I had"' (Bhana et al., 2021, p. 64).

In trying to understand Senzo's reasons for leaving ECE, there are three interdependent explanations which rely on the intersection of gender, race and cultural norms.
Firstly, Senzo experienced peer pressure and family pressure to perform a more traditional type of masculinity than the unconventional role of teaching the very young.

Secondly, Senzo is drawn to working with older students, teenagers. This may be because he feels more able to express his strong political leanings in his teaching with them but this is interrelated to reinforcing gender and cultural norms which provides prescripts about how to be a 'real man'. A third explanation is that he feels misunderstood by his female colleagues who cannot understand the pressure he is under as both a male and a person of colour.

Critical question

How far is it possible to empathise with and support a person who appears to come from a very different background (is of a different gender or race)? Use this question for a reflective discussion with trusted peers/colleagues and be really honest about your experiences!

So far, the discussion and illustrative material has focused mainly on the inter-section of gender and race. However, there are other key dimensions of difference which might feature in practices and policies aimed at the diversification of the ECE workforce. For example, the **heteronormativity** of the ECE environment has attracted much criticism (Blaise, 2005; Cloughessy & Waniganayake, 2014; Warin, 2018). Plaisir et al. (2021, p. 99) add social class structures into the mix pointing out the intersectionality of racism, homophobia and social class experiences for male workers in ECE. Regarding the intersection of age and gender it is worth mentioning the work of Kenny Spence in Scotland, who organises 'Men in Childcare'. Spence, manager of an ECE setting in Edinburgh, has dedicated himself to increasing the numbers of men coming into ECE. He has campaigned to attract men into this work through qualificatory courses held in evenings and advertised in local newspapers. The men can maintain an existing job whilst tasting ECE work and gaining the relevant qualifications. Consequently, he has had particular success with older men who choose to change career, sometimes after becoming a father or when friends and relatives have pointed out an ability to get on well with young children. Whilst the difference dimensions of gender, ethnicity, sexuality and age stand out in a consideration of ECE workforce diversity, it is also crucial to consider other social categories of difference that may be under-represented such as disabilities and religions.

Why Is It Important to Diversify the ECE Workforce?

There are several answers to this question depending on who we see as potential beneficiaries of a more diverse workforce. One answer stresses the importance of creating equal opportunities for minority groups to enter into the rewarding and meaningful work of ECE. Another is that the ECE setting will benefit as an orga-nisation through the expansion of practices, skills, interests and the range of mutual learning opportunities that are broadened when we work with others who appear to be a little different to ourselves. Everybody can benefit especially if a very varied workforce is managed in such a way as to maximise the range of skills and interests that are present. However, the most important group of beneficiaries is undoubtedly the children themselves. How do they benefit from a diverse workforce?

In the same way that children need a varied diet of food, they also need to come across variety amongst their adult carers, teachers and friends. Variety increases opportunity – opportunities for learning. Being exposed to different sorts of people increases the scope of social and relational learning. This is not to undermine the value of a continuous relationship with one key attachment figure, usually in the form of a keyworker, where the child's emotional stability and well-being is at stake. The ECE environment needs to balance the potential for attachment but also allow for exposure to different types of staff.

Another reason that is often presented for diversifying the ECE workforce rests on the assumption that children need role models since the modelling of positive behaviours by adults for children and young people is a deeply implicit aspect of child rearing and education. This idea is often presented as an argument for diversifying the ECE workforce, but it is a contested reason and one I consider to be problematic. Let's look critically at this assumption. Of course, children and young people, and adults too, have people they admire and want to emulate but quite often these may not be *positive* role models. When practitioners and policy-makers talk about role models, the 'positive' element is usually taken for granted and not enough attention is given to the attributes that are desirable for adult carers and teachers to demonstrate and the subtle values that are passed on through their conduct. For example, the UK Teacher Standards (DfE, 2021a) presents an implicit role modelling principle within Part One: 'Teaching' where are told that a teacher must 'demonstrate consistently the positive attitudes, values and behaviour which are expected of pupils' (p. 10). However, this document does not elaborate on the meaning of this bland statement.

We need to examine the theoretical roots of the role model idea. It belongs to the body of influential research and theory based on observational learning known as 'social learning theory'. Decades of research based on Bandura's famous Bobo doll study (Bandura et al., 1961) has revealed the influence of observational learning, demonstrating how children learn social behaviour by watching others. Developments of this body of research has focused on the characteristics of those who do the modelling, and these studies tell us that the young child is more likely to imitate those who have significance in their lives (Artino, 2007). Critics of social learning theory, especially those relating it to young children, suggest this approach does not lay enough emphasis on children's own agency and capacity to interpret the behaviour of the adults and reproduce it through their own understandings and creativity (see MacNaughton, 2000). These critiques do not deny the power of imitation, but they elaborate and nuance the rather simplistic view of one-way imitation. The attributes and positions of 'role models' are important too. Those who are recognised by young children as powerful may be more likely to be imitated. I learnt this in observations of young pre-schoolers' role play games of families with some very bossy, parental behaviour being imitated by young children with great vivacity: 'Go to bed! Go to bed right now!', accompanied with finger wagging, directed at several naughty babies. Teachers are especially likely to become models for children because they combine the two attributes of role models that are identified in the literature: familiarity due to the amount of time they spend with children (Brownhill et al., 2021); and power.

It is unsurprising that the concept of the role model has been widely used in discussions about the value of attracting more men to the Early Years workforce. It has been expanded to include damaging ideas about role model matching, for example matching male children to male teachers. The assumption behind this practice is that the male teachers will automatically demonstrate some kind of 'masculinity' (that the male child is deemed to be lacking) and that male children will automatically copy them. The assumption is that this kind of behaviour cannot be provided by female teachers. It is very problematic and leads to a reinforcement of gender roles rather than maximising men's presence in ECE as way to disrupt traditional gender roles and bring about a gender flexible pedagogy. This brings us to the specifics of the *gender* diversification of the ECE workforce.

Gender Diversification. Focusing on Gender. How Many Men and Who Are They?

I have already noted that the English DfE workforce strategy recommended the diversification of the ECE workforce but limited the idea of diversification to an exclusive focus on gender. Whist the report could, and should, have focused on other missing social categories, it came as a pleasing shift to see that, at last, the government was giving some serious attention to the low numbers of men in the workforce, stating clearly: 'we want men to choose to work in this sector' (p. 24). One of the report's recommendations was to create a task force specifically for developing strategies to recruit and support male members of the workforce. I was fortunate enough to be a lead member of the task force although sadly, our recommendations and our report (DfE GDTFG, 2018) like so many similar government initiatives, was not taken up or developed, except for a small amount of funding for a relevant conference. However, I succeeded in gaining funding from the United Kingdom's Economic and Social Research Council (ESRC) to lead a study that was specifically aimed at providing research to improve policy and practice on the recruitment and retention of man in ECE. This was the **Gender-EYE project**.

The project, based in England from 2018 to 2020, was undertaken through collaboration with nine different ECE case study settings, conducting a survey and gathering interview data with key stakeholders (Warin et al., 2020). One of the initial aims was to undertake a ground clearing exercise to determine how many men were, at that time, currently in the ECE workforce and also to examine who they were with regard to age, qualifications, routes into the profession and duration of service.

How many men ARE there?

At the time of commencing the study in 2018 three UK reports had recently attempted to identify the numbers of men working in ECE. The DfE report on the workforce referred to above claimed that 'From 2008–2013, the proportion of male staff in the workforce has remained consistently low at 2%' (DfE, 2017b, p. 24). A report by Bonetti (2018) presented the figure as 3% male (see Warin & Wilkinson, 2021). The overall picture created by these reports was that the proportion could be described as 2/3%. Compared with similar caring professions in the United Kingdom where the proportion of males is also very low, such as nursing, adult social care, social work and primary school teaching (Warin & Wilkinson, 2021, p. 4), it is clear that the ECE workforce is 'the least gender diverse of the caring progressions'. The figure of 2/3% is much the same across the globe. An OECD report (2018) claims the figure is no more than 3%. Commenting on this picture Warin and Wilkinson point out that:

> …it seems extraordinary in an age where there has been an increase in gender awareness, or at least much noise in social media about gender issues, to find this pocket of practice that appears to be so strongly gendered and so resistant to change. (p. 3)

The GenderEYE project sent a 'speedy survey' to managers of ECE settings to ascertain the numbers of men currently on the payroll who worked directly with children, establishing a figure of 4.4%. This must be qualified by recognising that the survey was probably answered by those who were already alert to this issue. We had to conclude that there had been little change and highlighted the 'stubborn resistance' of this pattern, also noted by Wright and Brownhill (2019).

Through interviews and a survey the study also set out to find out more about the nature of the male proportion of the workforce at this time. Who were the men employed in ECE? How were they qualified? How old were they? How had they come into the work? How long did they stay? We found that a pleasing 90% of practitioners held a specific Early Years qualification and we also found that there was no gender difference in level and type of qualification. Similarly there was no gender difference in the overall age profile of the workforce with a third of the men reported to be under 25, 11% in the over 61 age group and the largest proportion in the 26–40 age bracket, an outcome that replicates findings about the age profile of the profession as a whole (Bonetti, 2018). We found that more men had come into ECE work as a second career: 61% of men had been employed in another job first compared with 50% of the female workforce, suggesting a more protracted route (consistent with Spence's understanding of the career-changing men in the Scottish workforce). We also found a gender pattern with regard to duration of service and long-term commitment to ECE (see Warin et al., 2020 for statistical detail). Our findings, from both the qualitative and quantitative data showed that men's careers in the Early Years are marked by movement with some intending to move into primary schooling, some interested in specialist areas such as 'Special Needs' and some interested in promotion to management. Male practitioners that were new to ECE (within 5 years) expressed greater interest in moving 'somewhere' although it was often unclear where. Many wanted to keep their options open and saw their current role as a stepping-stone. We concluded that men's careers in ECE seem less stable than women's.

We have presented our disappointing overall finding about stasis in the employment of male practitioners as 'the 2/3% paralysis'. This result can be interpreted through another finding from the GenderEYE study. We found an absence of explicit strategy with the Early Years sector as a whole and within individual settings 'to really challenge and tackle this problem' (Warin et al., 2020, p. 8). For example, our interview data, including with careers personnel, revealed that boys in school receive very little exposure to ECE as a potential career. Consequently, there is a 'blindness' about the possibility of this career choice. An Early Years teacher trainer we interviewed made the following point:

> Quite honestly, men will not come unless they're invited. They're not going to come, unless there is more of an effort. We are attacking it the wrong way. We're not inviting them in. We're not putting them off, they were never put on in the first place. They never thought about it. (Warin et al., 2020, p. 9)

The lack of effort to challenge the gendered pattern of staffing is reflected at national governmental level (for example in the lack of serious follow-up to the 'Gender Diversification' section of the 2017 Workforce Strategy), and at the level of most providers too with the exception of a few gender champions who are taking significant steps towards recruiting men (Warin et al., 2020). Recruiting and retaining men requires resources and time which are scarce during a period when the sector is facing so many challenges. It also requires a clear rationale to galvanise activity, a point that became a key focus in the GenderEYE training package which was delivered to ECE managers and other key ECE influential people within the sector.

The GenderEYE toolkit and training sessions were designed to promote the recruitment and support of men, created and delivered in collaboration with the **Fatherhood Institute** (FI) our project partners. The package included such strategies as: looking for opportunities to reach out to men; involving existing staff; conducting open days; providing the right kind of imagery; creating male-friendly recruitment materials (with special attention to job adverts); supporting male recruits through support strategies, for example mentoring, 'buddy' relationships and support groups. We included a section on the role of 'positive action' a strategy that is permitted under the Equality Act to welcome applicants from unrepresented groups, usually women or applicants from black or minority ethnic groups. We were aware that this strategy had been very successful in Norway whose ECE workforce is currently 9% (see Warin et al., 2020 for further detail). We found there was some recognition of a 'values-based recruitment' approach which paid less attention to the applicant's CV and qualifications but which looked at their values, and potential for developing as teachers especially if the setting incorporated an apprenticeship route. This was explained by one female manager in the following way:

> Our recruitment team know that an agenda we have is, any males you get in, let's interview them. Let's not just take them on paper value … Because sometimes we'll get a CV through and it will just say that they've been a delivery driver and they've done a bit of retail. They haven't had childcare experience but there's obviously a reason why they're applying for this role within a nursery. So let's delve into that a little bit deeper. (Warin et al., 2020, p. 8)

One strategy that was adopted in the training sessions was to ask searching questions about the reasons for wanting to recruit more men. This brings us to the next section of this chapter which invites questions about the *value* of recruiting more men to the workforce.

The Value of Adult Male Role Models

In developing a gender flexible pedagogy, we need a clear rationale for increasing the presence of men. This is why it is important to examine underlying theories about gender (see Chapter 1). Theory determines people's actions and shapes policy and everyday practices. For example, if the theoretical rationale for developing efforts to recruit and support men is based on 'gender essentialist' ideas about differences between men and women, then the practices we see will be shaped by this view. In a setting pervaded by assumptions about what is 'natural' for men and women, it would not be surprising at all to find that male practitioners are deployed in outdoor play and excluded from nappy changing. Indeed, this is exactly what the GenderEYE findings revealed: the presence of hidden, unconscious, but influential theories about the value of men's presence in the Early Years workforce.

The GenderEYe training toolkit (Davies et al., 2020) introduces the 'Men in the Early Years' (**MITEY**) Charter which aims to steer away from recruiting men because they might bring special masculine qualities and, instead, promotes an inclusive workforce. David Wright, a very committed advocate for the 'more men' agenda created the MITEY charter as a tool to welcome men into ECE settings, often displayed prominently in their reception areas.

┤ Case study ├

Development of the MITEY Charter

The words of the charter have been carefully and subtly altered over the years with additional input from the Fatherhood Institute (FI). The later version which we have used in the GenderEYE toolkit compares interestingly with the earlier version from 2016. Here are the two versions alongside each other for comparison.

National Men in the Early Years Charter 2016 (from Wright & Brownhill, 2019, p. 193)

- Male carers, workers and volunteers are welcome.
- It is normal for boys and girls of all ages to be cared for by men and women.
- We recognise that children benefit from interactions with men and women and that both genders have complementary roles in caring for and developing them.
- We are seeking a balanced workforce composed of both men and women.
- We promote and support Early Years teaching as a career for both genders.

National Men in the Early Years Charter 2020 (from the GenderEYE Toolkit, Davies et al., 2020, p. 4 https://gendereye.files.wordpress.com/2020/10/gendereye-toolkit.pdf)

- We value men's capacity to care for and educate children, both within families and as professionals.
- We value the benefits to children of being cared for and educated by a diverse, mixed-gender Early Years workforce.
- We acknowledge that Early Years education should benefit from the talents of all, so we are actively seeking to create a workforce that includes men, women and people with other gendered or non-gendered identities.
- We are committed to removing the obstacles that stand in the way of a mixed-gender Early Years workforce, including low pay and status, limited career progression and gender-discriminatory treatment.
- We view Early Years education as a critical context in which to address gender inequality and stereotypes, for the benefit of children and wider society.

Critical question

What do you think has changed between these two versions of the MITEY charter? You might like to pay particular regard to:

- The underlying ideas about the **complementarity** of men and women in ECE versus ideas about their **interchangeability** (see discussion in Warin, 2017)
- The use of the **gender binary** to phrase the key statements

---

The idea of complementary versus interchangeable gender roles, introduced in the above exercise, forms a key theme in the next chapter where these concepts are explored more deeply.

Conclusions

- Pedagogy is a powerful word to describe the work of the ECE sector, focused on the whole child and their relationships. Consequently, it can encompass ideas about the gendered nature of teaching and learning for this age group.
- Diversification of the ECE workforce has been recommended but there is insufficient policy and research on race and other dimensions of difference that intersect with gender.
- However, there are good pockets of practice which adopt an intersectional approach to developing a workforce to represent a setting's wider community.
- The percentage of men in the workforce is still extraordinarily low. Recruitment and support strategies require much more effort and could benefit from the training strategies provided by the GenderEYE project.
- A strong rationale for the recruitment and support of men in ECE is vital for a really gender flexible pedagogy.

This last important point is taken up in the next chapter which examines how we attribute value to the presence of men in ECE. In advocating a gender flexible pedagogy a key question in this book is about how male teachers can act as a catalyst to create a gender flexible pedagogy, breaking down **gender stereotypes**, dismantling the gender binary, and showing the next generation that men and women can undertake the same roles.

━━━ REFLECTIVE QUESTION ━━━

- How far should male ECE practitioners be pro-actively recruited and supported?

━━━ READER CHALLENGE ━━━

If working in a professional ECE setting, make use of parent and community networks to invite a male representative of any of the community's under-represented minority groups to visit and read a story or undertake an activity with the children.

5

A Versatile Workforce

Introduction

Versatility goes hand in hand with diversity. It is crucial to the formation of relationships with a diverse group of young children and **ECE** colleagues. In this chapter, the emphasis is very much on the 'flexibility' part of the overall concept of a gender flexible pedagogy. It links ideas about the versatility of the ECE practitioner, an aptitude that is important to this sector, with ideas about *gender* versatility specifically. Given that much of my recent research has concerned the recruitment and support of male ECE practitioners, the main aim of this chapter is to consider how far the presence of male teachers can act as a catalyst for creating a gender flexible pedagogy. I draw on my ethnographic study of **Acorns** nursery, the recent **GenderEYE project**, and the **Swedish study** to illuminate reflections on this question.

This chapter looks at who does what within ECE exploring the nitty gritty of everyday practices. It examines how gender is implicated in the allocation of staff roles and responsibilities and how it influences the minutiae of behaviour such as choices about physical appearance: hairstyle and clothes. Key questions are: How far are men's roles and responsibilities gendered and constructed to complement women's roles and activities? How can men, and women, resist being 'pigeonholed' according to ideas about a **gender balance** within the workforce? How far are men's and women's roles interchangeable? How can staff deliberately disrupt gender through the explicit modelling of gender-atypical choices of activity and appearance.

I commence with a discussion about the threats of 're-gendering' ECE through the employment of male practitioners and consider how a concept of 'gender balance', as a rationale for mixed gender staff teams, implies a *complementarity* of male and female roles. I suggest that, instead, a rationale based on an *interchangeability* of roles is preferable and likely to lead to a greater gender flexibility. However, drawing on data from the GenderEYE project, I show that although managers and practitioners pay lip service to the idea of male and female role interchangeability ('everyone does everything') in reality gendered practices have a way of sneaking in. I then consider the demands of ECE for staff versatility and playfulness, and how these attributes are connected to gender flexibility.

Maintaining Gender Flexibility. The Risks of Re-Gendering the Educational Environment

I regard myself as an advocate for recruiting and supporting male teachers in ECE. However, I have argued (Warin, 2018, 2019) that there is an inherent risk in the employment of more men in ECE; a risk of simply reproducing traditional gender roles. In the illuminating work of Connell (1987, 1997) we gain insight into the ways that 'hegemonic masculinity' has a tendency to re-assert itself and undermine the best intentions of teachers and policy makers to transform the traditional gender order. Current interest in **unconscious gender bias** also reveals how subtle (and not-so-subtle) manifestations of gender bias creep into the best attempts to transform gendered practices. Sometimes ECE practitioners who believe passionately that they should challenge **gender stereotypes** find that in the minutiae of everyday practices they inadvertently recreate them. A nice example is the primary school teacher Graham Andre. He set out with a very generous openness to have his classroom televised for the **BBC2 TV documentary *No More Boys and Girls: Can Our Kids Go Gender Free?*** (2017) (see Chapter 1). The aim was to discover how far the children he taught could maintain gender flexibility and be 'free' of gender (Rycroft-Smith, 2020). His own unconscious sexism was revealed and discussed in the TV programme and indeed his learning from this 'difficult' and 'mind-blowing' experience (as he has described it in Rycroft-Smith, 2020, p. 11) led to his increased commitment to gender consciousness raising. We know from such instances and from the work of Connell that a 're-gendering' effect is very powerful and very difficult to prevent. This should not put us off but means we should try all the harder!

The term 're-gendering' and its opposite 'de-gendering' have been coined by Martino and Rezai Rashti (2012). A re-gendering of society emphasises the assertion of a traditional **gender binary** whilst a de-gendering implies moving beyond the gender binary. Researchers have pointed out that the inclusion of more men in the ECE workforce can actually contribute to a re-gendering of society, resulting in *more* rather than *less* gender stereotypical behaviour (Francis & Skelton, 2001; Haywood & Mac An Ghaill, 1996; Skelton, 2001). This is evident in some ECE settings that employ men especially when settings employ men and women to complement the attributes of others in the workforce. This can easily become a gendered process leading to an entrenchment of gender roles within ECE with male practitioners are deployed to undertake traditional male roles.

There are many ways that men can be stereotyped within the workforce. For example, they can be labelled as: disciplinarian, sports person (physical play), and provider of 'rough and tumble'. Indeed, the research on men in early childhood settings contains many examples of pedagogic practices in which men and women are positioned as different to each other in the contributions they bring to the nursery environment and their interactions with the children. For example, there is a large literature about men's contribution to rough and tumble play premised on the idea that this is the exclusive territory of the male practitioner (Fletcher et al., 2013). Simon Pratt-Adams (Burn & Pratt-Adams, 2015) provides an autobiographical account of the way he was expected to be a 'good disciplinarian' (p. 4). Others emphasise men's distinctive contribution to outdoor learning (Emilsen & Koch, 2010; Moser & Martinsen, 2010) and to sports specialism (Cushman, 2008).

The case study below is based on the GenderEYE project, presented in the previous chapter, and carried out from 2018 to 2020. It is adapted from our end-of-project report, and is based on an interview with a female practitioner in one of our ECE case study settings.

Case study

The story of 'Risky Pete' told by ECE practitioner Manuela Thomas (Warin et al., 2020, p. 14)

Manuela compared her current ECE setting with one where she had recently worked, criticising the headteacher in this previous setting for employing one particular, voluntary, member of the staff team.

There was a guy, but he wasn't an employed member of staff - they employed him for risk, to provide risk [. . .] he had a nickname. He was like Risky Pete or something. It was like a gimmick. That's an example of how this headteacher worked. So 'look at us, we've got Risky Pete'. Risky Pete had been in the Special Air Force (SAS) and like... we had a fire the other day at nursery, and I set it up and it was all done like that. He did a fire, and he didn't manage it properly and a child was burnt. And then this big SAS guy was too frightened to tell the parent so went to one of the female staff to get them to deal with it...Wouldn't take responsibility for it...But if you have a fire, if you've been trained in Early Years and how to do a fire, before you even set fire to anything you explain the rules. And that whole bit had not happened. It's just come to me, he was Dangerous Dave.

Manuela clearly felt that her own professional expertise and training in fire-lighting had been side lined in favour of the 'big SAS' guy.

Critical questions

1 What does this story tell us about the risks of re-gendering the ECE environment?
2 What does this story reveal about bravery and fear in relation to gender roles in ECE?

We do not know the reasons why the head teacher in this story selected this ex-SAS man to work in the setting. We can only imagine that this rationale has been fed by popular public ideas around the need for father figures in ECE to perform traditional male practices to compensate children who are missing men in their lives (Warin, 2018). The headteacher is also likely to be influenced by two popular public discourses. One of these is about the value of 'risky play' for children whilst the other is a problematic discourse about the potential contribution of ex-military personnel to teaching.

Risky play is argued to be a positive experience for children allowing them to develop resilience and work out their own assessments of physical dangers. This is particularly associated with the new value for outdoor education, and an increase in forest schools and their associated practices such as fire-lighting and tree climbing. In my ethnographic study of Acorns nursery and its five male staff (Warin, 2018), I was interested in finding out if male practitioners, compared with women, were expected to let children take more risks in potentially 'dangerous' situations such as climbing on play equipment or trees, engaging in 'rough and tumble play' balancing on beams and braving bad weather. Acorns' manager Rosie made the following comparison:

> [when] they're doing some physical development, balancing on beams and things… the females will tend to, that nurture instinct kicks in a bit more and they will walk beside the child offering a hand in case they need support for balance whereas the male will run along to the end and say, 'Run to me now'. And automatically say to the children 'It's safe. It's OK. You can do it. I'm waiting for you'. Whereas the female staff would possibly tend to nurture that little bit more'. (Warin, 2018, p. 105)

Rosie's view that men promote children's physical confidence through a greater tolerance of risk is widely held (Wright & Brownhill, 2019) and perpetuates the idea that male practitioners have a specific, gendered, contribution to children's physical development.

The second popular discourse that is very likely to have influenced the engagement of Risky Pete is his 'glamour' as a macho ex SAS figure. Interestingly and relatedly, the English '**Troops to Teachers**' policy introduced in 2012 (for a gamut of reasons including the rehabilitation of ex-military personnel) was intended to provide male role models to children especially boys. This was a time when 'boys without fathers' were seen to be a threat to society, as voiced for example by PM David Cameron in 2011 to explain the riots by young English people in that summer (see account in Warin, 2018). It was felt that ex-military personnel working as teachers might compensate for a perceived lack of 'discipline'. In actuality, the initiative was found to have very little take-up and has recently been scrapped altogether. Mallozi and Galman (2016) discuss the American equivalent 'Troops to Teachers' policy with the story of Tim, a white male US ex ex-marine in his twenties. They show how the US female staff exaggerated the exceptionality of male staff in

ECE suggesting that 'among school care-workers (in US ECE) the hegemonic form of masculinity continues to be embraced with vigour as men and women seek to demarcate difference [gender difference] in the starkest terms possible' (p. 53).

It would certainly seem that the headteacher in the account of Risky Pete is influenced by a strong gender essentialist gender discourse (see Chapter 1) which emphasises gender difference and is likely to result in a re-gendering. Contrast this headteacher's approach with the response of a manager, also in the GenderEYE project, who responded to our questions about gender influences on staff roles in the following way:

> Everybody is on exactly the same job description. Everyone's employed as an early years practitioner. Some have different accountabilities or responsibilities which they do. You know, like group leader or learning journals or that sort of thing. But no, everybody does everything. (Warin et al., 2020, p. 12)

This manager clearly subscribes to the idea of men and women being interchangeable rather than complementary in the roles they perform in the ECE.

Interchangeability of Roles and Practices. Gender Balance or Gender Flexibility?

I have articulated the concept of a '**gender flexible pedagogy**' in ECE partly as a reaction to the insistence on a value for ECE workforce 'gender balance' that I encountered amongst several colleagues who, like me, were researching the inclusion of more male practitioners. I also came across the gender balance argument amongst the participants in my ethnographic study of Acorns nursery.

Several members of the Acorns staff expressed the importance of 'balance' when explaining why they felt it important to have a mixed gender workforce. For example, Adam told us that children need to have both the male influence and the female influence in their lives to replicate the traditional family gender pattern: 'It is nice to have them both in here… Daddy… Mummy'. Craig reported that having a mixed gender workforce was important because 'you just need that balance'. The men's justifications for the promotion of more ECE men rests on a **heteronormative** idea that a male influence and female influence complement each other in raising children. These two practitioners are implicitly extrapolating from traditional heterosexual two-parent families to express a value for gender balance which they implicitly interpret as a complementarity of influences in ECE just as in the family. This is questionable. We know that families come in many forms, that LGBTQI+ families and single parent families co-exist with heterosexual two parent families. We also know from research undertaken from the late 1990s (Golombok et al., 1997), that girls and boys raised in lesbian-headed families, without the presence of a father-figure, were not disadvantaged with respect to their overall development and wellbeing. The concept of 'gender balance' is heteronormative.

We can see why it is so important to have a clear theoretical rationale for recruiting and retaining more male practitioners. An implicit idea about the complementarity of male and female roles will simply lead to a reproduction of the traditional gender order. It will mean that male practitioners are allocated, or choose to take up, childcare aspects associated with fathering whilst their female counterparts perpetuate classic mothering behaviours and practices. These behaviours will then be noted and normalised by the new generation of young children.

I have made efforts in various places (Warin, 2018, 2019) to assert the importance of having a clear rationale for the recruitment and retention of more men in ECE and have suggested the need to have a clear 'script' for this purpose. I have juxtaposed two possible scripts, one based on a perceived need for gender balance and the other, the preferable script that I am promoting in this book, based on gender flexibility. In contrasting these two scripts I take the reader back to the theories presented in Chapter 1.

The 'gender balance' script is underpinned by **gender essentialism**. It asserts gender differences and assumes there are 'natural' roles for men and women to adopt based on biological differences and the traditional aptitudes that have become associated with these. In a setting that practices according to this script it would not be surprising to find that male practitioners are allocated to physical play and excluded from care-focused practices such as nappy changing.

The gender flexible script has its roots in post-structuralism and **queer theory**. In Chapter 1, I explained that queer theory and post-structuralist theories of gender present a challenge to theories that are based on strong binaries such as male/female and self/other. Many feminists have embraced post-structuralism because this underpinning intention to deconstruct boundaries is directed at gender-focused binaries in particular. A gender flexible approach is nicely represented in the statement quoted above from one of the GenderEYE managers who describes the ECE job description as 'everybody can do everything'. A policy of staff interchangeability is a form of gender flexibility.

In a culture where 'everybody does everything' how do roles get allocated? At Acorns, Rosie the manager described her nurture of particular contributions that some staff bring to the ECE environment:

> And we want males to progress and if males, the same as females, have got a skill that they bring to us, like Steve with his guitar, we run with it, we embrace it with him, we invest in him. (Warin, 2018, p. 500)

ECE practitioners are employed to fulfil the professional job description expected of an ECE practitioner, regardless of gender. However, as Rosie indicates there is plenty of scope across an ECE staff team for specific skills and roles to emerge. These are constructed in relation to each other as part of the team dynamic. Acorns nursery was unusual in having a staff of five male practitioners at the time that I undertook my ethnography. In a minority of one, as is often the case in ECE settings where men are employed, the male practitioner has much scope for positioning himself in a predictable and traditional male role. However, it was fascinating to observe how the five male Acorns practitioners jostled for positions with each other to determine their own specific contributions to the settings. For example, Craig was upfront about his ambitions for a leadership role, relishing opportunities for his career development, whilst Chis quickly acquired a reputation for physical play, sports, and the outdoor area. These are 'typical' male roles as identified in the research literature (Emilsen & Koch, 2010; Francis & Skelton, 2001; Williams, 1995). The men's own personal strengths and aptitudes were constructed in relation to each other as well as to the women. Ben found this more of a struggle and in some respects his position as a practitioner in a nursery with other men who had appropriated the traditional male roles may have led him to the interesting gender-flexible identity that he created, and which will be described more fully below.

The idea of an interchangeability in men's and women's everyday practices is fine in theory. However, as we have seen, there are subtle, gendered forces at work influencing the realities and actual practices that emerge. This is exactly what we found out in the GenderEYE project (Warin et al., 2020): the existence of a strong 'interchangeability rhetoric' (everyone can do everything) co-existing with an undercurrent of gendered practices.

Consistent with the 'everyone can do everything' approach we found out from the GenderEYE survey that 83% (n = 105) of managers of EY settings reported that they always assign the same tasks to both male and female practitioners. However, when we scratched this surface principle the picture became more nuanced – and more gendered. In our survey for practitioners, there were significant gender differences regarding the frequency that men asked to undertake specific tasks in comparison to women. The most striking perceived differences were in:

- Nappy changing/intimate care (men felt they were asked to do less)
- Managing children's behaviour (men felt they were asked to do more)
- Lifting, carrying, and moving things around (men felt that they were asked to do more)

This pattern seems to confirm that traditional male tasks are alive and well in the ECE setting even when there is a rhetoric of interchangeable roles. Our survey for managers (n = 158) asked managers a question about the frequency of tasks performed by men with options of 'often', 'sometimes' and 'rarely'. Managers selected four categories for whom the 'rarely' option was found to be over 10%:

- Helping children with naptime (11%)
- Nappy changing/intimate care (12%)
- Writing reports/assessment of learning (13%)
- Tracking learning (10%)

Changing nappies or changing light bulbs?

We found a tendency in staff teams for men to do more of the traditionally 'paternal' tasks from risky play to changing lightbulbs and moving furniture, while women did more of the tasks that mirror a traditional maternal role like nappy changing, comforting of upset babies, and cleaning up. Many Early Years practitioners view gendered task allocation as 'natural', entrenching the idea that women and men are fundamentally different.

We were especially struck by the findings about nappy changing and nap time. We know that men can be put off work in ECE because they are worried they will be subject to accusations of paedophilia (Eidevald et al., 2021; Jones, 2004; Sumsion 1999), and that the area of touch between men and children, especially nappy changing, is a site of fears and moral panics (see Warin, 2018 for discussion and relevant research). However, we also know that ECE settings have rigorous safeguarding strategies and procedures, and that safeguarding is part of the ECE professional's training. We featured this finding in the GenderEYE training toolkit with the aim of developing awareness of how gendered practices slip into the work of ECE staff. The following extract is based on the **MITEY** (Men in the Early Years) Guide to Communicating with Parents about Male Staff which we included in the GenderEYE toolkit (Davies et al., 2020, pp. 7/8).

Case study

When male ECE practitioners don't change nappies (based on Davies et al., 2020, pp. 7/8)

'To limit men's involvement in certain aspects of the job of being an Early Years practitioner is to undermine their capacity to care effectively for children.

Changing nappies and soothing upset children are tasks that involve important emotional and physical work, and involve bonds of intimacy and trust between adults and children. It has been claimed that 'world peace starts on the changing table', and we support the recognition that underlies this quote, that attention to the bodily aspects of Early Years education is important. If only women are permitted to experience and engage with this element of the job, we set them up as the 'lead caregiver' and men as something lesser/different.

We believe that excluding men from the 'dirty work' of nappy changing, and other traditionally 'nurturing' roles, positions men in the Early Years sector as more naturally suited to 'educator', rather than 'caregiver' roles; tasks which are also more highly valued. This leaves women to pick up the 'female' tasks that have been so undervalued for so long; we think that's deeply problematic and needs to be challenged.

Critical questions

1   Do you agree with the statements above?
2   Are there other areas where men are more likely to miss out on key elements of Early Years practice?
3   What about women - what do they miss out on?

An important element of the work we undertook in the GenderEYE project was to assemble an image bank of drawings and photos of men undertaking ECE work. We had been disappointed at the lack of images promoting the gender atypical aspects of the work and had noticed that images used in publicity for the recruitment of more men portrayed stereotypical masculine interpretations of ECE work such as outdoor pursuits. We worked with a photographer and an illustrator to remedy this. The GendeEYE image bank can be found on our project website at: gendereye.org. This includes the image reproduced below, taken by photographer Rebecca Lupton.

Case study

Photograph of a male ECE practitioner at work (from the GenderEYE project)

Critical questions

1   In what ways does this image challenge and/or confirm gender stereotypes?
2   What would the advantages be of using this as publicity material to attract male recruits to EC? Any disadvantages?

For obvious reasons, we could not include a photograph of nappy changing in our image bank although we do have a relevant drawing created by our illustrator. The male practitioner depicted in the photograph above represents men's nurturing roles in several ways through the doll play and his relationship with the children close to him.

Gender Playfulness and Versatility

Versatility is a significant attribute of the ECE teacher. In England as in many other countries, as we have already discussed in Chapter 2, the Early Years Foundation Stage (EYFS) enshrines a pedagogic principle for responding to the needs of the 'unique child'. This principle 'leads logically to a **pedagogy** that emphasizes staff versatility as practitioners need to be able to respond sensitively to a diversity of children's needs' (Warin, 2018, p. 33). Yet it is not always easy to remain versatile and open to 'ways of being gendered that do not regulate but are *full of possibilities* for girls, for boys and for their teachers' (MacNaughton, 2000, p. 3, see Chapter 1). How can men, and women, resist stereotypic labels based on ideas about a gender balance within the workforce? People get stuck with roles, pigeon-holed by others but also by themselves. This tendency reflects a strong underlying essentialist theory of identity which assumes we have 'natural' characteristics, 'hard-wired' into our brains and inherited at birth or developed through a 'personality' or fixed identity. Feminist post-structuralists such as Glenda MacNaughton ask us to challenge this way of thinking in ECE. The versatile ECE teacher is a practitioner of **feminist post-structuralism** in action.

Men's presence as a catalyst for changing gender stereotypes

So far, we have considered how men's presence in ECE can actually work in ways that re-gender and reproduce the gender order, unless they and their colleagues and managers are on the lookout for re-gendering tendencies. We have looked at the allocation of staff roles in ECE and noted that this is one way that gendered practices sneak in to the ECE environment. We have especially noted that men may be excluded from, and may exclude themselves from, ECE work such as nappy changing and comforting children. So, what can ECE settings do to harness men's presence as a catalyst for challenging gender stereotypes? What can male and female practitioners do to make the most of male practitioners for modelling gender-atypical behaviours and practices?

A focus on **gender-sensitive** choices about physical appearance and clothing is one such way that has emerged in some of the research I have undertaken. This is an area where men and women can playfully and experimentally make choices about their own appearances that challenge children's growing 'gender rules'. Clothing and hairstyles have a strong visual impact on children. When trusted adults make dramatic changes to their appearance this is noticed, discussed, can be the source of fun and appeals to children's sense of humour.

For example, in the GenderEYE project one of our participants, a male practitioner in one of the case study settings, recognised that he was in an opportunistic position to challenge gender stereotypes. His rarity value as a male gives him an added bonus compared with his female colleagues for challenging gender stereotypes especially young children's growing alertness to 'gender rules' concerning appearance.

> One of the things I definitely felt in the early years classroom was that I was able to challenge gender stereotypes and assumptions in a way that was possibly easier than for my female colleagues. So, on purpose I would do things like wear pink ties because I knew pretty much every time that it would be commented on by a child and it would open up a discussion about clothing and gender, that kind of thing, which as I've discovered is still very deeply ingrained culturally. (Warin et al., 2020, p. 14)

At the time that I conducted my ethnographic study of Acorns nursery there appeared to be a trend for 'glitter beards' and this was a topic that was discussed when I attended a self-support group for men working in the Early Years. The decision to wear a beard but to decorate it with glitter (as Christmas festivities were in hand at the time of this discussion) seemed to combine traditional male and female elements of appearance, representing a gender flexible appearance, and at the same time, creating a sense of fun and playfulness around matters of dress and style, disrupting gender.

In my study with Swedish male pre-school teachers (Warin, 2016) I tackled matters of physical appearance head on. I wanted to see if the male pre-school teachers would open up about how they decided to get dressed in the mornings. To what degree were they making deliberate choices about what colours to wear, hairstyles, facial hair, and jewellery? Karl, for example, told me that he was able to challenge the children's gender stereotypical perceptions through his own physical appearance. He had recently engaged in a discussion with a 4-year-old boy who had told him that 'Boys don't have long hair' to which he had indicated his own shoulder-length hair and asserted 'Well I do!' Karl had described his views to me about the importance of **gender fluidity** and he presented his appearance choices as a deliberate gender-conscious practice. He believed his combination of earrings, beard and long hair presented a gender flexible appearance and disrupted traditional gender scripts. The other Swedish pre-school teachers were playful but also quite cautious in their choices about appearance. They would only go so far. For example Linus chose to wear pale purple shirts but would not wear pink. Jonas discussed the ways he challenged gender stereotypes in the classroom, (in keeping with the Swedish curriculum prescription to do this) by pretending to be a princess in a tiara. However, he also told me he would not go as far as putting on a princess dress. Similarly, Per told me that he would never come to school in a dress, not even to challenge gender because it 'wouldn't fit my personality. I wouldn't be comfortable.'

Why is it so very uncomfortable for men to wear dresses? How come dresses are so gender-threatening for males? In the late 1990s, I presented 50 4/5-year-old boys with a pink frilly dress to put on and assessed their reactions. This was an element in my PhD study to examine how children develop a sense of self as gendered when they commence formal schooling at age 4/5 (in the reception class in the UK system). So, 50 boys were presented with a pink frilly dress to put on – if they wanted – and I recorded their responses. The most illuminating element of the study was the preparatory phase for this as I had to determine, first of all, what clothing young children might consider to be strongly gendered (Warin, 2000). I learnt that there was no clear-cut choice for girls but for a boy the choice was easy – a dress. I learnt that there is nothing so gender-threatening as a dress. Why?

I discussed this question with Fran Cambridge Mallen who leads the UK campaign **'Let Clothes Be Clothes'** (2022). 'There is so much animosity' said Fran, to the idea of a boy wearing a dress or a skirt. We speculated about the reasons for this and agreed that 'If society has a problem with boys wearing dresses and skirts it is because of misogyny and homophobia' (recorded Zoom conversation, 07.10.2021). Fran used to run a business which made dresses and skirts for boys (depicting dinosaurs) attracting a social media following from parents who found that many boys were delighted with them.

However, the child who is happy to wear a dress in his nursery setting also needs to learn as he gets older that there are contexts where eyebrows will be raised at this behaviour (Warin et al., 2020). In the GenderEYE project, we agreed that young children need an element of 'metacognition' about challenging gender stereotypes. As they get older, they are likely to encounter more and more resistance to gender stereotype reversals. The GenderEYE data also included an account of an unusual practice in one of the project case study settings where practitioners wanted to challenge the 'gender rule' about men never wearing dresses. They felt that whilst their children were sometimes beginning to see male practitioners in princess dresses (due to the gender flexible practices of the setting) they wanted to broaden out to the include other examples of men in dresses. So, they decided to invite drag queens into the nursery on one occasion to read stories and to celebrate the visual impact and drama of their flamboyant hyper feminine clothing. This is a very creative example of gender playfulness. The organisation Drag Queen Story Hour (dragqueenstoryhour.co.uk) runs storytelling sessions for young children to capture:

> the imagination and play of the gender fluidity of childhood and gives kids glamorous, positive, and unabashedly queer role models. In spaces like this, kids are able to see people who defy rigid gender restrictions and imagine a world where people can present as they wish, where dress up is real.

Imagery is so powerful. I was recently invited to scrutinise a range of European pre-school picture books for the frequency of depictions of male staff. One Swedish book, 'Tisdags – Piraterna' (Tuesday – Pirates) by Edfelt and Johansson (2012), was especially noteworthy as it showed two gender-ambiguous adult teachers, for example one was wearing a baggy pink sweatshirt over defined breasts, track suit pants, medium length hair and a beard. These ECE professionals were depicted in the background of the story as a normal element of everyday pre-school life.

Gender switching at Acorns nursery

We have seen, above, that Adam from Acorns nursery implicated a gender balance principle of complementary gender roles in the belief that children need both a male and female influence – Mummy and Daddy. However, the five men at Acorns, between them, also represented a much more gender flexible view of their work in ECE. For example, practitioner Steve made the following interesting statement which nicely represents the gender flexible Early Years practitioner and argues for the importance of versatility. He believes that mothering and fathering can be practiced by one gender flexible individual:

> You can't be too stereotypical towards your own gender. It's just doesn't work. You can't be the masculine man. You can't be the feminine woman. Neither of them would work in this situation... It's aspects of both... It gets combined... Being a mother and father at the same time. You have to be able to do both. You can't rely on someone else to be the other half or anything because the same person wouldn't always be there. None of us work alone here **you've got to be able to switch** [author's emphasis]. (Warin, 2018, p. 33)

Steve implies that a restricted idea of gender roles could actually prevent an ECE practitioner from using the highly flexible range of skills that are needed for work with young children and emphasises a capacity for switching. Adam too emphasized his enjoyment of the versatility and adaptability needed to work with young children: 'we can do everything from, nappy changing, running, playing, teaching science...'. Ben also presented an idea of gender flexibility as part of his positive description of job satisfaction within his work. He told me 'I work here because... I can be whoever I want to be'. Of the five male practitioners at Acorns Ben appeared to embody and practice a notable degree of gender flexibility in response to the children. In the case study below, I have included several statements from my interview with him to demonstrate his gender flexible perspective.

─── Case study ──

Ben's gender flexibility (adapted from Warin, 2018; Chapter 3)

Ben had taken on board the very strong child centered discourse of preschool ideology which was linked to his enjoyment of the versatility of the job. For example, when I asked him about the possibility that some male practitioners become 'father figures' he rejected this idea right away and said:

I could be any figure they needed me to be. It's all on the children. But if a certain child just needs that extra person to bond with and have the rough and tumble time and play football, then I'm more than happy to give it. But more than happy to give cuddles as well and read stories.

He proudly portrayed the extraordinary variety of roles and skills that are required by the typical nursery practitioner:

There are some days when I'm in the garden building dens, building pirate ships, building trains, building princess boats. There are other days where I am sitting down reading stories. Other days where I'm putting the children to sleep. There's other times I am doing some painting ... There has been other days where we've been making jewellery. It's whatever the children want to do and how we can develop that activity and supply what they want to do.

Ben discussed his gender flexibility further and his words below suggest that individual practitioners can behave in 'both' ways. He is implicitly using the idea here of a gender binary that separates, one supposes, male from female behaviour ('both ways'), but he is also clearly acknowledging that he has the confidence to challenge the gender binary through his dressing up practices which he reinforces verbally with the children:

we got all these fabrics out and I started dressing up like a pirate. And then I put a flower in my hair as well and all the children said 'Pirates don't have flowers' and I said, 'Well this one does'. 'Boys aren't allowed to wear flowers'. 'Well this one does' ... or the other day I was Rapunzel and they all plaited the back of my hair... They just think it's funny because **they're seeing the both sides of what everyone can do** (male worker with 2–3 age group).

Ben implied that the ECE practitioner is a chameleon like figure who will change colour according to the child's lead. He is not constrained by traditional gender roles and this enjoyment of versatility in ECE pedagogy is linked to a capacity for gender flexibility.

Critical question

What do you imagine the main barriers are likely to be for Ben to 'practice what he is preaching'?

Remember that the above statements are made in an interview with a researcher (myself) who has an agenda about challenging gender stereotypes so Ben may be making statements that are designed to please. We have seen in this chapter that a rhetoric of gender flexibility and a principle of interchangeability are easy to talk about but not so easy to practice.

The data from Acorns show some evidence of male practitioners challenging gender stereotypes, through using their own gender flexible behaviour. We also heard about practice from some of the women in challenging gender stereotypes in a similar sort of way, for example dressing up in knights' armour or performing superhero roles. Their accounts of their gender flexible practices nicely illustrate the ideas expressed by Butler, evoking gender as a 'free floating artifice' (1990, p. 6) that can be variously performed by men and women, boys and girls, according to the demands of their socio-cultural context at any one moment in time.

Both male and female ECE staff can deliberately disrupt gender through demonstrating gender-atypical choices of activity and appearance and behaving in gender flexible ways. In this chapter, we have touched on some of the most gender-atypical ECE practices that men can potentially model: changing nappies, playing with dolls and wearing dresses.

Conclusions

- A concept of gender flexibility is more gender-transformative than a concept of gender balance as a principle for recruiting and supporting more male staff to create mixed gender ECE staff teams. Gender balance scripts can lead to re-gendering rather than de-gendering.
- A rhetoric of gender role interchangeability is easy to preach but not so easy to practice. Gender influences have way of sneaking into even the most gender-sensitive practices.
- A gender flexible pedagogy can be enabled through the presence of male teachers but only if they and their female colleagues are open to gender flexibility and versatility.

━━━━━━━━ **REFLECTIVE QUESTIONS** ━━━━━━━━

- How might the presence of men reinforce rather than challenge gender stereotypes?
- How can the presence of male ECE practitioners act as a catalyst to create a gender flexible pedagogy?

━━━━━━━━ **READER CHALLENGE** ━━━━━━━━

Change your appearance in the most gender-bending way you can think of, for one whole day, and record comments.

Section III

The 'How' of a Gender Flexible Pedagogy: How Can It Be Put Into Practice?

6

It's All About Relationships

Introduction

The previous section of this book, Chapters 4 and 5, considered the 'who' of a **gender flexible pedagogy** and presented discussion about the diversity and versatility of a workforce in the Early Years sector that has the potential to deliver this kind of **pedagogy**. In this next section, comprising Chapters 6 and 7, our attention turns to a consideration of the 'how' of a gender flexible pedagogy. We will consider how a capacity for gender-sensitivity can be developed and we will focus on the importance of human relationships within Early Years settings and their wider communities. We will build on earlier ideas about what pedagogy means and explore how it is a fundamentally relational concept.

The aim of this sixth chapter is to develop the concept of a gender flexible pedagogy arguing that it incorporates a value for relationality, care and human connectedness. I will emphasise how the Early Years in the United Kingdom and across the globe has always combined elements of education and care. I will discuss how this is not simply a one-way, top-down form of care focused on children as the receivers of adult care but how, crucially, the Early Years sector can be focused on developing young children as citizens who care for and about each other. This chapter is influenced by theorists who place the concept of mutual care and relationality at the heart of their educational visions emphasising children's caring for each other as well as care directed at them (Noddings, 2005; Warin & Gannerud, 2014). They emphasise mutual care rather than autonomous individualism as an endpoint of education. However, the possibilities of mutual care are influenced by gender, sometimes in ways that constrain its practice. I will open up questions about how gender influences teacher expectations about their own caring roles and responsibilities in their Early Years professional work as well as, most importantly, children's capacity to care for each other.

This chapter is structured by presenting the different kinds of relationships that exist in the ECE: peer relationships; adult/child relationships; staff team dynamics; relationships with parents. We will examine how these different types of relationships are mediated by gender. The chapter will also examine how early childhood education settings can work with families to challenge **gender stereotypes** and model an openness to, and acceptance of, different kinds of families.

Each section discusses these relationships with a focus on two main guiding questions:

• how gender mediates these relationships
• how the relationships can be managed to develop a gender flexible pedagogy

At the same time the chapter maintains an ongoing discussion about the development of relationality per se – how to develop children's own relationality and caring for each other as well as the care that is directed towards them in their relationships with **ECE** professionals (and other ECE adults).

Relationality

I begin by discussing relationality and mutual care. 'Relationality' is a mouthful but crucial and relevant word for describing the connectedness between two or more people (or non-human things). It emphasises human relationships and can be contrasted with a focus on individuality in discussions about educational purposes. Statements about educational purposes which have promoted the flourishing of the individual have been rife within educational policy-making during the last three decades. During this time (which spans my career in education and educational research) I have become increasingly critical of educational ideologies focused on the individual self-fulfilling person with underlying assumptions that each individual is free to 'choose' who to be. An over-emphasis on the development of an individual identity often pre-supposes that individuals exist in a social vacuum that exists independently of their social relationships and it also assumes there are no structural constraints on people's choices. I am sympathetic to the views of Layard and Dunn (2009) about the 'excessive individualism' rife within Western education which forms a key building block of neoliberalism (see Chapter 1). A recent book on neoliberalism in early childhood education (Roberts-Holmes & Moss, 2021) reveals its pernicious influences within this sector. They support a comment by Monbiot (2017, pp. 29–30) that neoliberalism is 'a vicious ideology of extreme competition and individualism that pits us against each other, and weakens the social bonds that make our lives worth living...', and they show us that this ideology commences in the Early Years Education setting. Whilst Roberts-Holmes and Moss' presentation of neoliberalism's impacts on early childhood education (ECE) is deeply concerning, these authors also include an element of optimism claiming that neoliberalism is 'resistible and is resisted' (p. 2). I believe that these possibilities of resistance lie in educational philosophies of interdependency and mutual care.

Mutual care

Hope and resistance can be found in expressions of educational purposes that are based on recognising the messy complexity of interdependencies between humans and that emphasise relationality, sociability and citizenship. For example, the following quotation from Fielding and Moss (2011) (discussed in Chapter 1) describes their educational vision as: 'a process of upbringing and increasing participation in the wider society, *with the goal that both the individual and the wider society, flourish*' (author's italics). They argue that 'this principle should inform both what we teach and how'. Their vision chimes with the ideas expressed by those educational visionaries who promote an ethic of mutual care as the heart of education (Noddings, 2005) which can be seen as both the ends and the means of schooling. Tronto's work in particular (for example in Fisher & Tronto, 1990, p. 41) unpacks the concept of care in considerable detail starting from her definition of care as inclusive of:

> everything we do to maintain, continue, and repair our 'world' so that we can
> live in it as well as possible. That world includes our bodies, ourselves, and
> our environment, all of which we seek to interweave in a complex,
> life-sustaining web.

This body of work, often described as the 'feminist ethic of care', presents a care ethic based on the realities of interdependency: the understanding that we are all receivers of care as well as care providers (Noddings, 1984, 2002; Tronto, 2006). To put it another way, human well-being depends equally on care giving and care receiving (Lynch et al., 2009). A resistance to neoliberalism lies in these ideas which present an alternative to the framing of educational purposes that envision the private autonomous successful individual as the endpoint (Warin & Gannerud, 2014, p. 196).

The message is quite simple. We need a pedagogy for young children which emphasises relationships and relationality and that is based specifically on reciprocal care. We need a pedagogy that supports caring *of* young children and caring *by* young children, respecting their own agency and capacity to care for others. To find this vitally important idea reflected in one simple image – look no further than the photograph displayed in Chapter 5. Here we can see both caring *for* the young child, in the way that the teacher is holding and playing with child, combined with caring *by* the young child, in the way the child is caring for the doll.

However, gender influences caring practices and policies in the ECE sector as in wider society, and we find that gender stereotypes are a barrier to this kind of pedagogy. The link between care and women's work exerts a subtle influence on gender stereotypes and expectations regarding the roles, responsibilities and behaviours we associate with men and women, boys and girls. How often would an ECE teacher deliberately choose a male child to comfort another who has fallen over in the playground? Might they perhaps intuitively choose a girl due to assumptions about girls having a more caring nature? Yet the ECE environment could be the very place to establish a greater equality of care or 'affective equality' (Lynch et al., 2009) where the burdens and benefits of care are shared equally between males and females.

If a gender flexible pedagogy is to be aimed at developing caring citizens as an outcome of a relational approach, then boys and girls need as much opportunity as each other to engage in caring activities and form caring relationships. Doll play is as important for boys as for girls, as is the care of pets and plants. Men's modelling of care is as important for children to witness as women's. The early years of education has the potential to be a site for a pedagogy focused on mutual care, understood as both a means and an end of education and freed from gender constraints.

Gender Influences on Children's Peer Relationships and How to Manage These

I now move on to develop this discussion about relationality, care and gender to examine young children's peer relationships. Two questions are key: How does gender influence children's peer relationships? How can peer relationships be managed to develop a gender flexible pedagogy?

The choices that young children make about who to play with are interwoven with choices about what to play with. Gendered patterns of play can emerge quickly in ECE with children's choices of toys and activities compounded by their peer choices (and vice versa). The classic stereotyped form of this is the recognisable pattern of girls clustering around domestic play and boys clustering around construction. In Chapter 3, I made the point that children's choices about activities are influenced by their choices about the people in the room. I presented a case study of an attempt by Swedish teachers to manage the resources in a Swedish pre-school class by distributing the domestic play equipment around the room to disrupt the gendered 'home corner' play that had developed. However, the attempt was thwarted by the girls' persistence in playing with each other at the same time as continuing to engage in domestic play – simply recreating homes in other areas.

In order to disrupt gender stereotypical ways of playing, ECE teachers will need to conduct some form of social engineering alongside their management of toys and resources. How far should they intervene in children's friendships to ensure that boys and girls have the opportunity to play together? Does it matter if they don't? As early as 1986, Smith pointed out that when a gender-segregated form of peer play becomes strongly entrenched then when boys and girls do eventually encounter each other at later stages there is a yawning gap in their experience and familiarity with other. They then approach each other as if from quite different cultures and may well have formed some disadvantageous stereotypes of the opposite group though 'othering' them which can sow the seeds for developing more extreme forms of prejudice such as misogyny. Thorne (1993) and Browne (2004) noticed that boys and girls largely play in separate groups engaging in stereotypically gendered activities. Building on this work Xu (2020) comments that 'Boys and girls divide themselves into oppositional groups that share different interests and play separately, and they gain their respective senses of being a boy/girl by referring to their same-gender peers and by distancing themselves from the opposite gender' (p. 358). Renold (2005) makes the important point that girl-boy friendships are often positioned by those around them as heterosexual with teasing about boyfriends and girlfriends. This creates an increasing barrier for children to engage in mixed gender groups and needs discouragement from ECE staff.

In some respects the issue for teachers of managing children's peer choices is similar to the concern previously discussed (in Chapter 3) about toy choices. In some ways it is very different. In that chapter we looked at strategic manipulation of toy choices by limiting their availability so that all children had to engage with the transport toys in the room, or with the domestic toys in the room. Some would argue that this kind of toy-choice manipulation infringes the important principle of child-centredness and that children should be as free as possible to make their own minds up about choices of activities and toys. This ethical dimension is even stronger with regard to teachers' interventions in peer choices. However, Early Years staff are often adept at some sensitive social engineering especially around children's emotional needs – for example deliberately finding opportunities for pairing up an isolated child with a sociable child. It may require some creative thinking to engineer and maintain mixed gender play and activities and resist the entrenchment of strongly set gendered friendship patterns. However, this is not beyond the capabilities of Early Years teachers and is vitally necessary to counteract gender stereotypes and create a gender flexible pedagogy.

Adult/Child Relationships

To continue the chapter's emphasis on relationships, I will now open up questions about how gender influences adult/child relationships in ECE and how adult/child relationships can be managed to develop a gender flexible pedagogy. I will consider: children's physical proximity to teachers in the classroom space; research on children's own perspectives about the relative importance of their teachers' gender; and will also briefly revisit the topic of gender-matching children to teachers and key workers (already touched on in Chapter 4).

Children's thoughts, and feelings, about their gender group membership was the key focus of my PhD study, carried out during the late 1990s. The context for this was the children's transition into Early Years education settings (pre-schools, nurseries and reception classes) and the study implicated many hours of observations (Warin, 1998). During these observations I became fascinated in noticing how children moved about their classroom space, indoors and outdoors, which other children they chose to sit next to or to play with and which members of staff they were most likely to gravitate to. How did gender enter into their sometimes deliberate and sometimes accidental relationships? I became particularly interested in the phenomenon I observed regarding girls' proximity to their female teachers. I recorded many instances of girls seated with at least one other female peer, engaged in tabletop activities such as gluing, cutting, drawing and positioned in close proximity to the female teacher who presided over these activities (there were no male teachers in any of the study settings). The choice of activity, choice of playmates and choice of engagement with staff all seemed to compound each other to entrench a pattern of female-focused behaviour for many of the girls. Whilst the study was conducted more than two decades ago, my more recent observations (in the **Acorns** study, and in the **GenderEYE project**) suggest that the pattern is often still present. Looked at another way, it seems that female teachers often collude in this pattern whereas, potentially, they could disrupt it, by undertaking more boisterous activities with the girls and at the same time finding ways to encourage the boys to take up the tabletop activities, be in close physical proximity and engage in talk with them.

Earlier in this book (Chapter 4), I discussed the practice of matching the gender of the child to the gender of the adult and how this idea applies to race as well as gender within a popular discourse about the need for specific role models. This practice is based on an assumption that young children are likely to develop a rapport with an adult who, visibly, shares key characteristics with themselves. Whilst this seems to be good practice and the expected pattern of rapport may indeed develop, it does require some care and an open mind. As we saw in Theresa Gilmour's account of her staffing strategy (in Chapter 4), a simplistic form of adult-child matching can be completely changed by a child who has their own preferences and forms relationships with adults in unpredictable ways.

What do young children themselves understand about the relative merits of male and female teachers? Do they notice? Do they care? Xu's study in Scotland and China (2020) used pictorial conversations with young children to access their insights on how far the gender of their teachers matter to them. He found that children do indeed notice the gender of their practitioners, usually linking them to their fathers and mothers. He also found that even for very young children their views reproduce traditional gendered behaviours such as men kicking balls, and women holding babies. However, in addition, he found that children's preferences regarding the gender of their teachers were not as important as their capacity to play and have fun with them, a finding reinforced in Hutchings et al. (2008) and research on older children's preferences too, e.g. Lahelma (2000). In England, the London Early Years Foundation (LEYF) conducted research to access young children's views about the importance of teacher gender. They found children commented that male staff were faster roundabout spinners and higher swing pushers than their female counterparts (O'Sullivan & Chambers, 2012). This work was followed up by Helen Perkins and Tracey Edwards (see account in Nurseryworld, 2018) who used pictorial methods, like Xu, to find out whether teacher gender was important to young children. Their conclusions are in line with Xu, suggesting that children don't have strong feelings about the gender of the teacher but are more concerned about the rapport they have with them and the teacher's expertise in various activities, for example 'I like playing football with her because she's good at it'. So, when teachers deliberately undertake gender atypical activities, they need to be good at them. For example, a male teacher friend has recently taken his own baby into his classroom both virtually, online, and in person. It seems likely that his expert care of his baby will have made a strong impression on the 4- and 5-year-old boys and girls in his class.

Staff Team Dynamics

In this section of this chapter, I ask how gender influences staff team relationships in ECE, and I consider how staff relationships can be effectively managed to develop a gender flexible pedagogy. I consider the support that is needed in staff teams who employ men and women together and the ongoing reflection and discussion that can be harnessed as rich gender awareness opportunities in mixed teams.

Many adults can be found in an ECE setting – many who have non-teaching roles, such as lunch time supervisors, cleaners, gardeners, and chefs, as well as volunteering parents. Some settings are adept at involving people in social inter-action with children and employ non-teaching staff with this in mind. Indeed, such interaction cannot be avoided in any case when socially gregarious and curious children initiate contact. During the GenderEYE study we were aware that it was important to incorporate these more peripheral roles in discussing the contribution that men can bring to the pre-school environment. For example, in one of the case-study schools a male cook was employed who also helped small groups of children with their own baking activities and meal preparation in addition to his main function to provide lunches and snacks. He developed a strong rapport with some of the children and was mentioned by staff in this setting as an asset. Such opportunities for interaction with some of these adults increase the social and relational learning potential in the setting and add to the richness of learning opportunities.

However, such opportunities may be missed. For example, during one of the observations I conducted in Acorns nursery, a be-suited male visitor entered the classroom. He had come to inspect the pipes in a corner of the classroom, with some kind of health and safety brief (I never found out the exact information about who he was). He slipped into the room like a grey shadow, undertook his business with no interaction at all with others in the room and slipped out again. Perhaps the teacher could have drawn attention to him and interested the children in the work he was carrying out. Perhaps he could even have been enticed to prolong his visit by a few minutes to chat with children and even read a quick story!

The Crucial Role of Leadership

There is much to be said about the crucial role of leadership provided by ECE managers in the promotion of a gender flexible pedagogy. This topic will be developed further, in the next chapter, in relation to the importance of creating a 'whole school' approach to gender flexibility and equality. In both the GenderEYE project and the study of Acorns, the researchers witnessed and heard about leadership dilemmas in relation to much-needed ongoing support of male teachers. The employment of male teachers carries certain responsibilities as these people are, in many respects, 'sticking their necks out'.

A particularly sensitive area of management practice and policy concerns how the setting manages men's 'intimate care' practices with children. Every setting needs a clear policy on this emotive element of Early Years work in relation to men's and women's roles and responsibilities (McHale, 2022). For example, in the Acorns study, we heard about a father's strong objection to having his young child's nappy changed by a male practitioner. The manager felt that every practitioner should undertake exactly the same professional duties within the setting ('everyone should do everything'), including intimate care. Yet she was also very sensitive to the father's viewpoint and recognised the need to develop trust over time between this parent and the male practitioner. After a very short period of time, during which the male practitioner did not undertake 'intimate care' duties, the father realised that a good rapport had developed between his child and their practitioner, and soon developed the necessary confidence for this male member of the staff team to undertake these responsibilities. McHale (2022) tells a similar story from her data which indeed include the parent apologising to the male member of staff after having an initial resistance to this practice. Sometimes managers develop a 'line in the sand' about this suggesting that a wary parent should simply find another setting in which women-only are allocated to intimate care duties. We found one such example in the GenderEYE project where the manager explained her approach to a parent:

> I had to have that conversation and say, all of my staff are DBS checked … There is no difference in our practice between male and female teachers. So, my male teacher, if needed during the routine of the day, will change your child's nappy. And then it is down to the parents to decide whether you're

going to stay at my nursery or you're going to leave my nursery, because we are an inclusive nursery and we are not going to, you know, treat our male or female teachers differently because of their sex.

Other commentators suggest a 'dialogue-based approach' between directors and parents is required based on an attentive listening to, and understanding of, parental concerns (Hedlin & Aberg, 2019). This form of quality leadership requires empathy and sensitivity to all the key ECE parties, balancing and negotiating the different needs of children, parents and staff as an interdependent set of relationships.

Another sensitive issue concerns the need for decisive leadership in relation to fears about 'dangerous' male staff – the potential for men to abuse and sexually abuse young children. Many male employees are fearful that their presence will be misunderstood arousing public and parental suspicion (Sargent, 2004) which sometimes materialises in actual allegations of sexual abuse (Sumsion, 1999). Indeed, in the GenderEYE project we found evidence that such fears are strong barriers against entry into the profession. In one of the GenderEYE case study settings we heard a relevant story that illustrated some of the difficulties faced by male employees in Early Years education and that had repercussions for the manager with implications for her leadership and promotion of an ethic of mutual care.

Case study

Story about the experiences of Kevin and Rob at Bowergate pre-school (pseudonym) from the GenderEYE project (based on Warin et al., 2020)

Bowergate pre-school had four male employees at the time of our study making it a particularly interesting site for our exploration of the value of a mixed gender workforce. The GenderEYE researchers heard about the following critical incident from one of the men involved in it and also from the manager.

Two of the male staff, Jason and Rob, had taken a group of children to play in a nearby public park. They were horrified when a woman, a stranger, angrily accosted them and asked them what they were doing with the group of children. After the men explained their professional roles she continued to express her disgust and hostility. This was very upsetting to the two professionals involved in this incident who then sought the advice of the setting's manager. The men had gained considerable relief from talking about this with the manager who treated it confidentially and sensitively. As a result of these conversations, the manager recommended that the men should attend a local support group for men in the early years. This particular support group had indeed been set up to provide a safe space for men to discuss such incidents as well as specific allegations, from parents and others, about sexual abuse.

Manager empathy and very sensitive support with such experiences is vital to prevent a knee-jerk reaction by employees to leave the professional world of ECE altogether. The men remained in post – but such hostility leaves a very deep wound.

Critical question

To what extent should this manager have used the incident to engage in a whole-staff discussion of such issues? How might this be managed?

In this example, it may well have been very supportive that the incident involved two male practitioners working together with the potential to give each other emotional support. A key element of a gender flexible pedagogy implicates the fostering of supportive relationships within the staff team concerning engendered aspects of ECE policy and practice and, when possible, encouraging open discussion of concerns.

Relationships With Parents

How does gender influence relationships between ECE staff and parents? How can these relationships be managed to develop a gender flexible pedagogy? I'll consider three points to answer these questions: how staff in ECE settings can respond to and work with a whole range of family types ensuring inclusivity; how parents respond to having a mixed gender workforce in their children's ECE setting; how parents can work with ECE teachers and children to challenge gender stereotypes.

Firstly, how can ECE settings adopt an inclusive attitude to parents? Within the points of practical advice that Price (2018) gives about gender diversity and sexuality in ECE, there is guidance about how settings can be inclusive in their practices with children's families. She focuses on the initial phase of rapport building between staff and parents – a crucial time for establishing that the setting is welcoming to all kinds of families. Price had noticed, in an online search, that the ECE induction 'All About Me' forms that were given to children's parents and carers often made use of two columns headed 'Mother' and 'Father' likely to cause discomfort for single parents and same-sex parents. By way of contrast, on a research visit to a Norwegian ECE setting I observed the inclusive practice of ensuring that the children's families, carers, parents and 'significant others' were represented in photographs on each child's personal locker space. These were hugely varied. The nursery staff had worked closely with families to determine which adults, siblings, grandparents and others should be represented there with choices influenced by the child. Same-sex parents were well represented as were grandparents and siblings.

A particular focus on ECE staff engagement with fathers has been on the agenda of the ECE sector in England since the rise of **Sure Start** and **Children's Centres** during the late 1990s and Early Years of the millennium. It was recognised then that it was enormously beneficial to young children to have fathers closely involved in their learning and a number of excellent practice models were developed at that time (Broadhead & Meleady, 2008; Chandler, 1998; Warin, 2006; Whalley, 1997). These practices were often, but not exclusively, based on the presence of male practitioners. In the Acorns study some of the male and female teachers I interviewed suggested that fathers sometimes find it easier to approach a male member of staff to chat about their child (see Warin, 2018 for further discussion of this point and more detail about research into male-led outreach work with fathers). A mixed gender workforce offers parents a greater breadth of potential points of contact with staff.

What do we know about how parents in general respond to mixed gender teams in ECE? Dissatisfied with out-of-date research findings, Wright and Brownhill (2019) managed to collect responses from 440 parents across a range of ECE settings in England using a short online survey. They found that there was overwhelming support (92%) for the employment of men in ECE. Objections from a small percentage were based on suspicion, a lack of trust and what one parent described as 'instinctive uncomfortable feelings'. Wright and Brownhill point out the powerful emotional language of mistrust that was used by a small minority of their survey respondents and suggest that strong feelings from this unsympathetic group can have a considerable impact. More recently, McHale's (2022) survey of parents has found a very similar pattern of positive support but also that the small minority of parents who do object, especially concerning 'intimate care', have a strong impact on men's confidence. Despite these influential exceptions the consensus from surveys is that parents can see many advantages to the employment of men.

In qualitative studies the benefits of men's presence are often described with great enthusiasm by parents. For example, the Acorns study (Warin, 2018), as an ethnography, allowed for a triangulation of observations of and accounts of responses to the five male practitioners that were employed in this setting including parental perspectives. The gender flexible practices of practitioner Ben, based on observations and interviews, have already been described earlier in this book (Chapter 5), so it was interesting to hear from a parent whose child was cared for by him. She recognised and valued his versatile multi-skilled practice:

> My daughter's world is composed of women and men, and girls and boys, at home and in the nursery. It is good that not all of the key people in her life are female. It is in fact positive that she sees that men are carers and teachers as well as women. As a parent I know that my daughter picks up on stereotypes very easily, and with [Ben] I note that she is a princess and a pirate.

This parent recognises that it is valuable for her daughter to behave in gender flexible ways, switching from traditional female stereotype role play to traditional male stereotypes and seeming to be comfortable with both – inspired and modelled by the gender flexibility of Ben.

The parent quoted above attached value to a pedagogy that challenges gender stereotypes. Parent respondents in the Wright and Brownhill study also made comments about the value of men's presence for challenging gender stereotypes and were glad that young children have the opportunity to see that both men and women can be caring. McHale's (2022) survey of parents found that 80% of her sample agreed with the statement that 'working in a caring profession allows male early childhood educators to challenge stereotypes about what it is to be male'. However, parents often express anxieties about gender non-conformity in young children and these are usually based on heteronormative assumptions and implicit fears about children 'learning to be gay'. These concerns are more likely to be focused on fathers' anxieties about their sons. For example a report from the National Education Union (Jennett, 2018) includes a comment that staff felt that fathers often worried more than mothers about boys 'acting like girls' and they cite a fairly relaxed response from a mother:

> In reception, quite a few of the boys wander around in aprons and things like that. One mum commented on this. She said 'I'm sure he's going to be gay' – but I don't think she was being negative. However, sometimes parents say that boys mustn't do this or that. (**NEU** report; Jennett, 2018, p. 8)

In the GenderEYE project (Warin et al., 2020) we tell the story of staff who regularly removed a Princess dress from one of the boys just before his father arrived to take him home. Homophobia and a fear of homophobic bullying exert a huge and often invisible influence on a resistance to challenging gender stereotypes. I've already discussed this in relation to the strong feelings that can be provoked about boys in dresses (Chapter 5) especially focused on paternal resistance to this behaviour. The following case study describes the content of an informative and moving video about a gender non-conforming child which I would encourage readers to look at for themselves. It was created by Cecile Cassel-Holly Siz, released in 2013 as video for the album 'My Name is…'. It presents a dramatic and ultimately satisfactory story about how one family comes to terms with the young child's gender non-conformity. At the time of writing this is available on YouTube from HollySiz.

━ Case study ━

Account of a father's response to his gender non-conforming child (based on Holly Siz video)

A classroom of young children (aged approximately 6/7 years old) are listening to their teacher read a story. We see sexual behaviour from a boy blowing kisses at a girl. This is observed by a child of indeterminate gender with curly black hair wearing a lilac-coloured dress. The teacher notes this child's look of gloominess. Next we see the same child, now no longer in his dress, putting on a denim jacket in the school hallway ready to go home.

We then see the child at home in front of a mirror now with the dress back on again twirling it around and smiling happily. We then see a playful interlude with 'My little Pony' toys, which are marketed as 'girls' toys. This play continues at the family dinner table where the child combs the pony's hair eliciting a smile from Mum and a glare from Dad. The father then seizes the toy and flings it on the floor. Mum and Dad argue. The child, who we now realise is male, looks miserable.

We see increasing hostility between parents. We also witness other boys teasing our protagonist by pulling his curly hair, behaviour that is observed by his father at home time. We see the father trying to play baseball with the child and we witness an interview where both parents have been called in to talk with the teacher. This ends with further parental arguing.

The next scene depicts the father sitting in the child's bedroom holding the lilac dress and deep in thought.

The final scene shows home-time again with assembled parents waiting to collect their children. Some of them are smiling and some not. Their gaze is directed at our young protagonist. Dressed in the usual home-time denim jacket the child approaches the waiting parents. The child's face suddenly lightens as he gazes towards Dad and we see that Dad is wearing a dress. Our protagonist rushes towards him and embraces him. The final shot depicts them walking away together hand-in-hand both in their dresses.

Critical question

How might this narrative be translated into an activity for ECE settings working with parents on gender. How far would this evoke sympathetic responses from parents? What sensitivities would have to be considered and how might they be tackled?

The **Gender Action** campaign works with staff teams together with parents and has developed a strategy for persuading resistant parents about the importance of tackling gender stereotypes. They point out that it is necessary as a form of anti-bullying groundwork. In a personal conversation with Georgina Phillips who spearheaded Gender Action she pointed out that parents are sympathetic to the argument that sensitive gender issues (for example same sex families) do need raising with children so that they have a basis of acceptance that all kinds of families are equally valid. The implication is that the bullying happens when the topic is silent and invisible.

Conclusions

In this chapter, I have promoted the idea of a pedagogy that is based on relationality and mutual care. However, this kind of ethic and vision within ECE can be obstructed through the playing out of gender stereotypes which confine caring to women and girls. The Early Years sector is a fertile environment for a deliberate and gender-conscious approach to reversing the gender stenotypes of care ensuring that boys and girls have equal opportunities to care for each other, for their environment and for those more vulnerable than they are. The ECE environment is one which can establish five related principles of a gender flexible pedagogy of mutual care and relationality:

- We are all providers and receivers of care.
- Care is both the means and ends of education.
- Boys and girls need equal opportunities to develop mutual care and relationality.
- Children will be more likely to develop an equality of care practices if they witness both male and female adults modelling care.
- ECE staff need to support children's gender non-conformity and provide sensitive support to enable parents to do the same.

REFLECTIVE QUESTIONS

- How far should very young children choose their own companions and how far should the Early Years pedagogue socially engineer their peer relations to enable mixed gender groups? What are the barriers?

READER CHALLENGE

Look up and engage with the organisation *Roots of Empathy*. This international organisation has a branch in the United Kingdom promoted by the Early Years. It aims to develop empathy in young children promoting behaviours such as sharing, helpfulness to others and inclusiveness. A key element is based on a regular visit by a baby and their parent (from the school community).

https://www.eyalliance.org.uk/roots-empathy-uk

7

Creating the Gender Flexible Early Childhood Education Setting

Introduction

This chapter explores ideas about **gender sensitivity** as a cornerstone for bringing about a gender flexible pedagogy. I discuss how a setting can develop this capacity, implicating the necessary idea of a 'whole school' approach. The chapter considers various types of training in gender sensitivity: interventions and initiatives from outside 'expert bodies', and in **continuing professional development (CPD)**. I also discuss the surprising lack of a gender-focused element of pre-service initial teacher training. Various gender experts have identified **unconscious gender bias** as a major obstacle to positive gender transformation. This chapter will discuss what this means, also considering the related idea of **gender blindness** and recognising that an unwillingness to tackle and transform gender essentialist beliefs can be found in many early childhood education **(ECE)** settings, just as in wider society.

There is a particular focus on developing a sensitivity to gendered language use in everyday practice as a manageable strategy for challenging gender stereotypes. I also include ideas about how a setting can create positive gender ripples that can impact on its wider community.

The 'whole school' concept

I begin with the story of a friend who is a male reception class teacher, Arun, currently working in a primary school in the London area. He is very aware of gender issues and very determined to challenge **gender stereotypes** in his reception class. However, when I chatted with him about his policies and practices, he told me about how his efforts are not always supported by other staff within the same organisation. In particular, he mentioned how the lunch time supervisors are still lining children up in the playground by gender group. This is not just a lack of support but a serious undermining of his efforts. What should he do? The answer lies in a 'whole school' approach so that everybody is 'singing from the same song sheet' and collaborating on a shared aim to challenge gender stereotypes.

A **whole school** focus is a fine idea in theory but very difficult to operationalise. It requires shared values and priorities across the whole staff team. I became attuned to dilemmas about staff team dynamics in relation to the 'whole school' ideal when I was evaluating the use of nurture groups in primary schools (Warin, 2017). In one of the target schools, I became aware of a silent battle between the staff who had been trained specially to run the nurture groups (by the Nurture Group Network [NGN]) and those who had not. The first group had a **pedagogy** emphasising empathy and understanding so that when children behaved poorly in class their behaviour was understood as a form of communication and a need for understanding from teachers and others. The second group, stressed through neoliberal assessment demands (especially with older age groups and all that rides on this for a primary school), had a very different set of aims and perceived poor classroom behaviour to be a major barrier to the children's academic achievements. Indeed, this school provided a very clear illustration of Ball's analysis of 'institutional schizophrenia' (Ball, 2003; see Chapter 1). What was required here was a 'whole school' educational philosophy, based on effective communication, to prevent each group undermining the aims of the other group. While this example has a different focus (on the nurturing/nurture group aspects of the school), the need for an integrated and consistent approach from the whole school community is exactly the same for challenging gender stereotypes with the same attendant dangers that some staff, unintentionally, undermine the efforts of others as in the case of Arun.

What does 'whole school' mean? A nice definition has emerged from the organisation 'Mentally Healthy Schools' (at the Anna Freud National Centre for Children & Families, 2022) who claim that whole school:

involves all parts of the school working together and being committed. It needs partnership working between senior leaders, teachers, and all school staff, as well as parents, carers and the wider community.

These definitions stress what we might also call the 'culture' of a school, its 'general ethos', ambience or 'ethic' (Warin, 2017).

However, the need for a whole school approach to certain particular educational aims has become an overused refrain. For example, the promotion of a whole school approach has been produced in relation to emotional literacy (Weare, 2004), an 'ethic of care' (Warin, 2017), anti-bullying (Anti-Bullying Alliance, 2022), restorative practice (Short et al., 2018), and children's social and emotional development (Goldberg et al., 2019). It might also be used in relation to sustainability aims, a value for play and creativity, children's health. Clearly, there is a problem as each of these single foci are worthy of becoming a whole school focus. Faced with this decision about the focus of a whole-school ideology settings must decide whether to be selective and prioritise one focus over another and/or find an all-embracing focus such as inclusiveness which can accommodate various foci such as gender as part of an intersectional approach. The debate here recalls the discussion in Chapter 2 which touched on how far gender should be an explicit part of the Early Years **curriculum** or whether it should be subsumed under the more generic banner of equality, diversity and inclusion (EDI). I believe that society needs some beacons of excellence where the focus is very specifically on gender and where the setting's institutional ethos has gender right at its heart, aiming to tackle gender differences that have a negative impact on children's well-being and their educational achievement. This kind of commitment is in line with government guidance on Gender Issues in Schools (DCSF, 2009):

> Tackling gender differences that have a negative impact on educational achievement is best done at a whole school level and as part of the institution's general ethos.

The Institute of Physics (IOP) has developed a very strong focus on gender, initially through its work on secondary school girls' opportunities for involvement in science, technology, engineering and mathematics subjects (STEM). Recently it has urged the importance of combating gender stereotypes with younger age groups lower down the school system (IOP, 2022) and developed a manifesto for change in schools and Early Years as part of its 'Limit Less' campaign (IOP Campaign, 2022). This has given rise to the organisation **Gender Action** developed by the Institute of Physics which accredits whole school initiatives that are aimed at challenging gender stereotypes. This award programme has different levels of accreditation for schools and nurseries who engage with its framework and resources: supporter; initiator; champion; beacon. Through this framework, there can be an identification of specific schools that are recognised as exemplary in the work they do to contest gender stereotypes.

The key to success in developing a whole school approach to gender awareness lies with leadership, that is to say the communication of clear aims to all staff expressed in and reinforced in various ways from written policies down to chats in corridors. It may start at the point of staff appointments where heads can deliberately appoint staff according to such expressed aims. However, 'leadership' can also come from an inspirational gender champion in the setting who is fully supported by the senior leadership team and who can carry the rest of the staff along with them (see the previous chapter for more discussion of leadership in inspiring a gender flexible pedagogy).

Examples of attempts to develop whole school approaches to gender

I will now present some examples of a whole school focus on gender. These are quite recent examples from the English context including findings from the **GenderEYE project**. In our GenderEYE research we asked managers and practitioners in all the case study settings to tell us what gender awareness training had been experienced, if any. Of our eight different case studies the most gender aware was one located in a city in the south of England, a city known for the diversity of its population especially the preponderance of LGBTQ+ people. The case study below is compiled from the interview and observational data collected in this setting.

── Case study ──────────────────────────────────────

Example of an effort to develop a whole school approach to gender: Sandyside nursery (pseudonym) (based on data collected in the GenderEYE project: genderEYE.org.com)

A number of features mark the setting out as being gender aware. The front door makes a point of welcoming 'all families' and a quick look at material in the office included the books *First Feminist Book for Boys* and *First Book About Feminism for Boys*.

Four practitioners highlighted recent changes in the provision of books. One had received Stonewall training (see Chapter 3) and explained its impact on relations with children and their families: 'accepting all the different families, accepting the children the way they are, potentially dealing with gender-fluid children, non-binary'. Consequently, the setting's resources were expanded, and the practitioner had purchased the book 'Julian is a Mermaid'. The same practitioner discussed problems in a previous setting especially her wish to use books about same sex parents (*My Two Mummies, The King and the King, And Tango Makes Three*'), saying 'I couldn't get those books in'. We also heard about a 'diversity walk' that had taken place at Sandyside to audit resources: 'Yeah I think we had someone come, I don't know whether it was part of the Council... she went through the whole nursery looking at our resources to see if we were diverse enough in all areas, you know in sexuality… obviously ethnic, you know different cultures and all of that. So then, so a lot of recommendations came out of that'.

We were also told of language-focused gender training from the city council and how a staff meeting had promoted the use of the pronoun 'they' with badges left for staff use if they wanted. This had then prompted further debate and conversations amongst the staff.

However, the level of staff engagement in gender-focused training was patchy. Two practitioners were hesitant about their experience of the relevant training saying, rather vaguely, that there had been some training in a staff meeting when a video had been used to trigger conversation about 'attitudes to gender', 'around race' and 'our own sorts of views and prejudices and things like that'.

Two points emerged about the gender awareness of this setting. Firstly, although there was clearly a positive level of gender training, especially the initiatives from the city council, it was apparent that this was not an explicit 'whole school' focus. As one practitioner said, 'It's an implicit rather than an articulated agenda'. Secondly, the practitioners, when asked why there was a degree of gender awareness within the setting, responded by referring to this setting's location in a highly gender-aware city, one claiming; 'It's X (name of city). I think it's very normal. It's just we live in this bubble and things are a bit different here'.

Critical question

The staff at this school explain the possibilities for gender awareness through the wider context of the city's LGBTQ+ culture. How far could the efforts evidenced here work in other towns and cities?

I have also gained insight into relevant whole school practice in conversation with Georgina Phillips one of the key people in the Gender Action campaign. This organisation, described above, has awarded 'Supporter' status to two nurseries in Southwark London who have taken on board the need to ensure that the whole setting is working to challenge gender stereotypes. In a presentation of Gender Action's work to interested parties at City Hall in London (Gender Action, Youtube, 2019), the nursery heads make inspirational statements about the impact of Gender Action but are also candid about the intractability of some staff. For example, one head says that while the staff have really taken the Gender Action work on board 'Some have been sceptical … saying' why are we doing this work? Another head says she's been surprised at how mixed the reactions of her staff have been including some who have found it 'quite challenging' necessitating support 'to understand why we're doing it and why it's important, and opening their eyes'.

The **Fawcett Society's** report (2020) discusses a number of 'whole school' initiatives that have taken place to challenge gender stereotypes in Early Years education. The report describes these as programmatic initiatives – which take place over time and work with the whole setting including parents. It features the work of two such interventions '**Lifting Limits**' and 'You Be You'. Lifting Limits aims to deliver whole school approaches to addressing gender stereotypes, working with a school 'gender champion' and commencing with an audit of relevant resources, policies and practices. The programme is delivered though staff **INSET,** workshops with parents and carers, and a package of resources which help 'to bring into the open, for discussion and challenge, gendered stereotypes wherever they are encountered' (Fawcett Society, 2020, p. 56). You Be You is a Key Stage 1 intervention (children aged 5–7 in the English system) designed on intersectional principles. The Fawcett Society's report informs us that its pilot phase resulted in a '32% decrease in the proportion of pupils who agreed that girls are kinder than boys' and a '46% increase in the proportion who acknowledge that it is Ok for boys to like playing house' (p. 57). These findings show evidence of a change in young children's gender stereotypes as a result of this intervention. Significantly, these changed stereotypes are concerned with the possibilities of de-limiting care activities making it more possible for both boys and girls to engage in mutual care, as discussed in the previous chapter.

Another programmatic, whole school, initiative was introduced by the National Education Union who developed their work 'Boys Things and Girls Things?' (Jennett, 2018). This was an intervention with five primary schools in England and Wales to consider how traditional gender stereotypes could be challenged in the classroom. A key feature of the intervention was based on staff training with the aim of improving staff gender sensitivity.

The above examples can demonstrate the value of one-off initiatives. This may just be a one-day INSET training or it may be a longer programmatic intervention. The most sophisticated models of gender sensitivity training provide a series of events and resources aimed to be used over time with a cumulative 'drip drip' impact, as recommended by Josephidou and Bolshaw (2020). There is much power in bringing independent 'experts' into the setting to inspire and motivate change. However, these initiatives all have a 'shelf life' in that the duration of the initiative is finite so they need to be complemented and supplemented through other means of gender transformation focused on staff training.

Implications for Staffing and Training

Staff training in gender awareness can come in many forms, occur in a variety of contexts, and happen at different stages of a professional career in the Early Years. In the next section, based on the English educational context, I identify three different forms of staff training: Continuing Professional Development (CPD) including one-off workshops and longer duration interventions; informal training within a setting managed through formal and informal staff meetings and discussions; staff training prior to teacher service as trainee teachers in Initial Teacher Training.

Continuing professional development (CPD) is a term which covers any kind of professional development while in post in order to improve professional capacities and abilities. It can range from INSET days (in-service education training) and what are often known as 'twilight sessions' which are specific teach-ins, workshops and meetings held for staff at the end of the school day. The examples of whole school approaches presented above all use a component of this kind of training opportunity which facilitate a sharing amongst all staff members so they can take joint ownership of goals and key ideas and, sometimes, as I will discuss below, develop a shared language.

Team teaching offers great potential for informal discussion and for the learning potential that is on offer when colleagues work in the same classroom and can act as 'critical friends' to each other. Within a trusting team-teacher relationship, there are rich opportunities for sharpening our gender-sensitive antennae. For example, co-teachers can tactfully point out each other's gendered assumptions and support each other to nip in the bud any gender stereotypical comments or forms of play that are communicated by the children. In the same way that I recommended a 'gender-sensitive opportunism' in Chapter 2, in relation to children's behaviours and practices, there is also a similar need for staff working with each other. For example, in the GenderEYE project we heard that some settings found the most useful kind of 'training' in gender sensitivity to be spontaneous staff discussions that arose in response to particular everyday occurrences of gender issues (Warin et al., 2020).

A gender flexible ethos is underpinned by a culture which promotes reflective practice. The development of critical approaches to the practices of oneself and others is a vital tool for self-development and improving our teaching to benefit young children. It can be done simply and spontaneously through good communication with colleagues especially where honesty feels safe, resulting in the 'critically reflective emotional professional' (Osgood, 2010). Josephidou and Bolshaw (2020, p. 154) include a down-to-earth discussion of what it means to engage in critical reflection as an Early Years practitioner, encouraging a synergy between asking questions about our own practices and promoting a questioning approach in the children we teach.

I now move on to a consideration of gender sensitivity training in initial teacher training **(ITT)**. If we are in the midst of a 'gender revolution' (see Chapter 1) surely initial teacher training should contain a strong element of such learning opportunities. However, the Fawcett Society report (2020) found a dearth of gender courses and sessions in the pre-service training of Early Years teachers. This report includes findings from a poll aimed at revealing how much training Early Years practitioners had been exposed to. The poll presented a definition of gender stereotyping and then asked respondents if they had received any training on challenging gender stereotypes prior to starting their current employment and also while in post. For 4 in 10 practitioners, training was limited to an occasional reference or was not present at all. This research also found that even fewer practitioners had received any CPD on challenging gender stereotypes within their current roles. Our findings from the GenderEYE project (Warin et al., 2020) showed a similarly low level of training opportunities for practitioners to develop gender awareness. Although the more highly qualified practitioners had sometimes had opportunities to explore gender stereotyping during undergraduate degree training there were few opportunities for exploring gender during lower levels of training (Level 1/2 in the UK qualification system). What is more we heard that training was sometimes based on essentialist ideas around men and women. For example one outraged male practitioner pointed out the gendered assumptions made by his course leaders:

> I did my PGCE at [X] University and there were about 120 people on the course and about ten men within that. Two of them were on the Early Years programme and the rest of us were general Primary, and I think they'd identified early on that we were a vulnerable group that needed support...I went along and...we were told this: 'Men or boys, you are not as good at paperwork, so you'll be supported with your files'. And I was thinking, right I will show you that my file is going to be the best [LAUGHS]. So, but I was a bit taken aback then by the assumptions that were being made.

What are the reasons for the dearth of training in gender awareness? Some evidence suggests that **ITT** trainers are anxious about delivering this kind of training. The **National Education Union** report (Jennett, 2018) found that the leaders in the five project schools reported that some staff felt uncomfortable with, and lacked knowledge about, challenging gender stereotypes. Other authors have similarly pointed out the difficulties of inducting students into critical approaches to gender (Hogan, 2012; MacNaughton, 1997; Warin, 2018). Sometimes this is based on their recognition of students' low value for this area of teacher preparation alongside student resistance requiring 'sensitive handling in order not to generate fear' (Drudy, 2008, p. 312). Another strong influence on the lack of relevant training is that teacher training concerned with the social aspects of children's development is squeezed out by the neoliberal influences discussed in chapter one and an increasing focus on helping children's early development of more 'academic' skills' – the skills that can be measured.

Concluding these disappointing findings about the lack of relevant training, the Fawcett Society authors suggest the need for government funding for a training package that could be delivered to nurseries and schools on how to tackle gender stereotypes, and should also ensure that challenging stereotypes is a focus of equalities CPD (Fawcett Society, 2020, p. 51). A number of academics and researchers who are interested in gender issues in ECE are also teacher educators for the Early Years and Primary School sectors. Some of them have written candidly about their struggles to engage students in critical reflections on gender inequalities and underlying gender stereotypes (for example, Josephidou, 2018; Lenz Tagucci, 2005; Mahoney, 1996). One such person is Yuwei Xu who has worked as a teacher educator in three different higher education institutions. I interviewed him about his experiences.

┌─ Case study ─

Reflections of a gender-focused teacher educator: Interview with Yuwei Xu

Yuwei began by emphasising the importance he places on gender sensitivity training and explained that he has 'always done a session about gender and how it matters' across the programmes he has delivered for Early Years trainee teachers on BA, MA and EYITT programmes.

His approach emphasises reflection and reflexivity:

I start with reflections from students themselves. These inform the discussion. Reflections are prompted by two key questions: In general how do you reflect on how gender matters in your work with children and young people? How do you think your gender comes into that?

Yuwei pointed out that some students start from the position that 'We are all gender neutral; we are all professionals'. He told me that the concept of gender neutrality had led to some heated debates. Often students had assumed that gender is unimportant until they start to reflect on current case studies ('things that are actually happening in 2022'). So Yuwei makes a point of using concrete examples derived from his research in England, Sweden, China and Germany to provide provocative case study stories (see Xu, 2021). For example, he tells the story of practitioner Jess, in England who:

> noticed that children's coat pegs in the cloakroom area were segregated into boys and girls and the nursery children had male and female icons on their registration name cards. She did not regard this as an issue until children queried whether a boy with longer hair was hanging his coat in the correct place – the children presumed he was a girl.

Yuwei also used a nice example of a planning activity in China where practitioner Pan:

> planned an activity with two roles: the bulldozers that destroy the blocks and the architects who help to build. Children were divided into two groups and took up one of the two roles respectively. Pan expected that boys would like to damage things and girls would like to help others. However, both girls and boys wanted to play to be the bulldozers.

Yuwei pointed out that teacher educators often have a mindset that is strongly impacted by developmentalists and developmentally appropriate practice. He believes there is a need to train teacher educators before they themselves can train students.

Critical question

What factors influence the paucity of gender awareness training in EYITT?

I now move on to consider a question about the form of training sessions in gender that has engaged me within my research on the employment of male practitioners in the Early Years. Is there a case for single-sex male training? Through various research projects focused on the participation of men in the Early Years workforce I have come across a number of single-sex male groups and courses as part of staff training in EYE. For example, Geir, a Swedish ECE educator I interviewed (as part of the **Swedish study**), felt it was important to offer this kind of support to his male students. More recently in the GenderEYE project we gave thought to the case for single-sex training and discovered that a small number of educational settings in the United Kingdom are providing all-male introductory training courses in ECE. We recognised the inherent problems of single-sex training, noting that it reinforces the gender binary. We concluded that such forms of training (and on-the-job support with other men) must be integrated within an overall emphasis on gender sensitivity training so as to prevent a reinforcement than a challenging of gender stereotypes. This brings me to explore the concept of 'gender sensitivity' in a little more depth, the term with which I commenced this chapter, and that has pervaded the above discussion and indeed the whole of this book.

The concept of gender sensitivity training

Josephidou and Bolshaw (2020) have written a lot about gender sensitivity training **(GST)**. They give some very specific advice about how to run **GST** in ECE – with advice tailored for whether the training/professional development is offered within a setting, is part of continuous professional development, or constitutes part of a programme in Initial Teacher Training. However, they make two points which apply to all the above training contexts. Firstly, they point out the value of a 'provocation' or stimulus in much the same way that Yuwei Xu (above) used his case study stories to trigger critical reflection. They make concrete suggestions for what these provocations might be such as an episode of the TV programme *Friends* which featured a male nanny, or the use of a music video (*Stupid Girls* by Pink) (p. 160). Secondly, and more importantly, they advocate that trainees in GST discuss gender issues at both a macro, societal level and also at a micro, individual level. For example, they might start by considering a macro gender issue such as the continuing existence of the gender pay gap and then hone in on their own personal experiences of feeling that their work is insufficiently recognised and rewarded. It can be rewarding to switch between a macro lens emphasising structural inequalities, and a micro personal lens turned inward to emphasise personal experiences of gender. This can develop personal gender sensitivity at the same time as a sensitivity to the political and structural influences on gender.

There is a consensus that gender sensitivity can only be developed by teacher educators who are themselves gender-sensitive, a point also made by Yuwei Xu above. Josephidou has written in detail about how she has tried to enable students' own reflection on their personal experiences by being honest about her own

(Josepehidou, 2018), a recommendation also made by Hogan (2012). Others also point out that the best approach to develop the necessary reflectiveness and critical reflection is most effectively modelled by teacher educators themselves who are willing to be quite open about their own personal learning and changed perceptions in gender-thinking. We need to 'turn the spotlight on ourselves challenging each other to consider any stereotypical thinking we may hold about gender' (Josephidou & Bolshaw, 2020, p. 154).

Unconscious bias and gender blindness

The opposite of gender sensitivity is gender blindness. In Chapter 1, I introduced this concept describing it as 'a disregard for the importance of gender as a mediating influence in social interactions'. According to UNICEF (2017) (cited in Josephidou & Bolshaw, 2020), gender blindness is a:

> failure to recognise that the roles and responsibilities of men/boys and women/girls are given to them in specific social, cultural, economic and political contexts and backgrounds. Projects, programmes, policies and attitudes which are gender blind do not take into account these different roles and diverse needs. (Josephidou & Bolshaw, 2020, p. 142)

Josephidou and Bolshaw are highly aware that there are many inherent problems in raising gender issues with staff. They suggest that people can feel attacked, become confrontational, adopt essentialist scripts or express positions based on patriarchal gender norms. They use the term 'gender blindness' to describe the lack of gender sensitivity that they encounter amongst many ECE student trainees and in-service teachers.

Identifying and explaining the concept of gender blindness can feel like creating a conundrum. If we want to move to a society where the **gender binary** is dismantled, or at least challenged, troubled and disrupted (Butler, 1999), then surely we don't want to focus on gender differences. Yet to pretend that the gender binary does not exist is not helpful either. We were very much aware of this puzzle in our findings from the GenderEYE project. We found that several staff in our case study schools wanted to claim that staff in their setting were treated exactly the same: that men and women can perform all the roles that are required of an Early Years professional in exactly the same way: 'Everybody is on exactly the same job description … everybody does everything' (Warin et al., 2020, p. 12). However, this rhetoric of gender equality, and sameness masks the existence of gender stereotypes in the Early Years setting and creates an image of a genderless professional. This finding from GenderEYE reinforces the findings of previous researchers on gender blindness amongst many teacher trainees (Hogan, 2012; MacNaughton, 1997; Mahoney, 1996; Robinson & Diaz; 2006; Warin, 2018). Gender blindness underlies teacher trainees' resistance to training in gender issues which they see as 'superfluous'. However, co-existent with this rhetoric, our GenderEYE data shows that gender stereotypes seem to have way of slipping into practices and language in the interactions between staff with each other and with children. This means that Early Years' staff, especially those in leadership roles, have to find strategies for unearthing these buried gender stereotypes and bringing them into the light. What is required is a way of attacking unconscious gender bias, revealing gender blindness and developing gender sensitivity. A detailed attention to our everyday language is one such approach.

Watching Our Language

A key element of staff training, in its various guises and at various stages of staff training and development, is on language. If we are to enable young children and the adults who bring them up to develop gender-sensitive antennae, we also need to help them focus these antennae on relevant elements of the world around them. Being sensitive to the language that we use ourselves, the language of children and the language of their teachers is a vital focus for the ambitious aim of challenging gender stereotypes.

A focus on language also seems a positive step because this is an area where change is actually possible and can happen at the micro-level of our everyday interactions. The genius of the campaign group commenced by Laura Bates to challenge 'everyday sexism' lies in its focus on the mundane prevalence of sexism in our lives which we can recognise and call out. While larger macro-level gender issues must be changed at the level of government policy (such as parental rights of leave) or international level (such as the UN Sustainable Development Goal to achieve gender equality), in our own everyday lives we can make small changes and language is the site where this is most possible. We can become aware of and then make changes in the words we use and the ways we use them. We have to begin by developing gender-sensitive antennae which picks up on our own behaviours and language practices and which hone-in on the gendered practices of others around us.

I began this book by mentioning an example from my own life as a parent (Chapter 1): I became aware, when I was a parent of young male children that I frequently referred to them as 'the boys' and I noticed a similar, unconscious, language practice in other parents. We were entrenching gender difference by referring, quite unnecessarily, to gender group membership of our children. This is a practice that is widespread in primary schools when teachers often find it necessary to issue an instruction to a sub-group of children in the classroom ('Girls: please do this'; 'Boys: please do that') even if more overt forms of gender segregation are not so evident. The **NEU** project referred to above (Jennett, 2018) has an emphasis on language in its work with staff. For example, one of their 'Points to consider' is

> Think about language used in the classroom. Little things such as substituting words like 'children' for 'girls' and 'boys' or 'parents' for 'Mums and Dads' can help to affirm the things we have in common rather than our differences. (p. 10)

Xu (2021) reports on data from a nursery in Sweden where a practitioner, Christian, noticed how a parent used markedly different vocabulary and a different tone of voice when talking to a girl and a boy.

> The parent pointed to a girl's sweater and said with a light voice: 'What a niiiiice sweater you have with cherries.' The parent then turned to a boy, lowered the voice and said: 'What cooooool letters you have'. Christian noticed the different tones and terminology used by the parent, where the boy was spoken to with a deeper tone and that he had a 'cool' sweater, and the girl got a lighter tone and had a 'nice' sweater. (p. 12)

As a result of noticing and discussing this incident, the setting decided to talk with parents about a need for gender-sensitive language.

Unconscious language practices became the focus of the interactions between primary school teacher Graham Andre and his young students in the ground-breaking TV documentary, referred to elsewhere in this book, *No More Boys and Girls: Can Our Kids Go Gender Free?* (Rycroft-Smith & Andre, 2020). Graham Andre is made aware that he uses sexist terms of endearment when addressing the children in his class such as 'Sweetie' and 'Love' for the girls and 'Mate' and 'Buddy' for the boys. The children are asked to keep a tally of the times he does this which creates wonderful learning opportunities in gender-sensitisation for both teacher and for children and, of course, for the TV audience. This is the kind of subtle language practice that we need to sensitise ourselves to so that we can 'catch ourselves out' every time we slip into these unconscious language habits.

The organisation Stonewall (whose work has been discussed at earlier points in this book) provides a specific resource on the avoidance of sexist language. This is not only aimed at those in education but at anybody who wants to become more gender-sensitive especially with a focus on the use of non-sexist language. Advice includes some of the points made above about removing unnecessary gendered words such as 'boys and girls' 'Mum or Dad' and also advocates the use of general non-gender-specific terms such as partner or sibling, and when addressing a gathering of people, use terms such as 'everyone' or 'folks'. The resource also gives guidance on the use of pronoun choices in personal introductions and signatures and recommends respect for the use of the gender-neutral pronoun 'they' (they/them/theirs) which some people choose to use.

Following up the points made above about the importance and relevance of our gendered language, Josephidou and Bolshaw (2020) point out that GST can bring about a new terminology and useable vocabulary. An example is the term '**heteronormativity**', the assumption that heterosexuality is the normal expression of sexuality. This word requires little definition in many circles especially within the LGBTQ+ world. However, it is opaque to some people. When I first encountered this concept, I realised it was about identifying a norm that had been invisible and unnamed to me beforehand. The identification of the concept made it visible and valuable. Josephidou and Bolshaw suggest that a new terminology can give people more confidence and enables them to speak with a louder voice to challenge and disrupt gender (p. 159).

The Interaction Between the ECE Setting and Its Wider Community of Families

It may seem far-fetched to suggest that an Early Years setting can have an impact on the values and beliefs of its wider community – yet such a thing is possible and indeed there were many fine examples of this kind of local influence during the 1990s under the auspices of the **Sure Start** initiative in England and the development of government funded **Children's Centres** (Eisenstadt, 2011). Many of these centres became beacons of help and hope especially for particularly needy children and their families with spreading influences on such things as healthy eating, and the value of outdoor play. It is quite possible that a gender-focused Early Years setting will cascade its influence to its wider community, creating ripples of gender sensitivity. The route for communication about gender values, especially challenges to gender stereotypes, is via quality staff/parent relationships (as discussed in the last chapter). In this book we have already heard the story of a father who was hostile to the nappy changing duties of a male practitioner in his young child's pre-school but who gradually changed his tune over time and established trust. Alongside this emotional change in his relationship with the practitioner is a change in his perceptions about gender roles.

An ECE setting that has a whole school approach to challenging gender stereotypes can take advantage of such spontaneous learning moments in relationships with parents. However, some centres are also in a good position to influence the values of their wider communities through specific events, open days, workshops and courses. The story presented earlier (Chapter 6) about public suspicion of two male practitioners with children in a public park shows just how important this might be so that gender awareness can permeate outwards from a gender-sensitive ECE setting. The case study below suggests one way that this might be done.

─── Case study ──────────────────────────────

The big pink photograph: Idea for a community workshop

I led a workshop for a 'community day' at my University, which was intended to showcase, in a fun and interesting way, some of the research ongoing at our institution. I decided to conduct a workshop on gender issues together with a colleague who was also working in gender-focused research. The workshop was entitled 'We can all do pink' and the participants included a mix of participants from the university's immediate community including parents, staff and children from the university's pre-school together with others from the city. We asked our participants to come dressed in pink clothing and accessories regardless of their gender. The event started off with a 'pink think'. With the aid of images drawn from a whole range of different sources we began by discussing how and, interestingly, *when*, the colour pink became such a signifier of the female gender group. For example, we looked at images of young children, boys and girls, dressed in pink in the 18th and 19th centuries. The culmination of the workshop was for everybody present to pose for a 'big pink photograph' and to be rewarded with pink treats.

It struck me afterwards that this would be an ideal activity for an ECE setting to undertake with parents and with their wider community – to get everybody involved in an unthreatening discussion of gender stereotypes and why they matter. This would nicely prepare the ground for a brief presentation about the setting's policies and practices on smashing gender stereotypes.

Critical question

How far can ECE settings act as utopias of gender flexible relationships and practices? What are the obstacles?

Conclusions

- A whole school approach is required in Early Years settings in order to deliver a gender flexible pedagogy. This is a challenging ideal but is the only way to prevent some staff undermining others in the achievement of an overall higher level of gender sensitivity amongst staff.
- Specific gender sensitivity training can be delivered in an ongoing way though **INSET** and **CPD** sessions, bringing about a 'drip drip' effect over time and can often be inspired by an external gender-focused organisation who can inject the necessary motivation especially with resistant and **gender blind** staff.
- However, we also need to see a much stronger presence of gender issues in the provision of training in ITT.
- Gender sensitivity training can also be brought about through the ongoing and spontaneous discussion of gender issues that emerge through all aspects of practice with the children and work with their parents and within staff team relationships.
- A specific focus on our uses of gendered language can be a particularly effective way of bringing about gender sensitivity.
- At its very best the policies and practices of a gender-sensitive staff team can have an impact on the setting's wider community.

━━━━━ REFLECTIVE QUESTION ━━━━━

- What gender blind spots are you aware of in your own professional or domestic life?

━━━━━ READER CHALLENGE ━━━━━

Ask a 'critical friend' within your professional setting, or a trusted family member, to record any sexist language you use, over a clearly defined time period, and feed this back to you.

Section IV

Conclusion

8

Last Words and Final Messages

Introduction

So this chapter is the place where I give a last word on the importance of a **gender flexible pedagogy** in the early years of education, and how it can be implemented. I draw together the content of the previous chapters and crystallise the preceding discussion into a set of takeaway messages about the **what**, **who** and **how** of gender flexibility in Early Years education. I also assemble some of the most thought-provoking strands of the book that give rise to unanswered questions and that are worthy of further debate. I end with a final call to action for Early Years academics, practitioners and policy-makers.

Achieving the book's aims

The book set out to promote the idea of a gender flexible pedagogy for the early years and to examine ideas about the resources, workforce and settings who can deliver it. I aimed to give a practical emphasis to the making of a gender flexible pedagogy with ideas to try out, stories to learn from and challenges to take up.

I structured the preceding content by looking at three related foci: concerning the *what*, *who* and *how* of implementing a gender flexible pedagogy. The book is also underpinned by a crucial question about *why* we should want to adopt a gender flexible pedagogy in education for the very young and what is lost to the world if we don't. I will take the opportunity here in this conclusion to open up this question in order to reinforce my reasons for promoting a gender flexible pedagogy. Firstly, I will summarise what I mean by it.

What is a gender flexible pedagogy?

The theory of gender flexible pedagogy (initially introduced in Warin & Adriany, 2017) draws on Butler (1990) to emphasise how early childhood educators, both male and female, can model a flexible approach to the performance of gender which disrupts prescriptions for men to model masculinities and women to model femininities. It incorporates ideas about the resources and activities that young children themselves may be encouraged to engage in, with an emphasis on playful and experimental approaches to the performance of gender which allow for gender transgression. It also implies the need for **ECE** staff to be gender-sensitive, through exposure to relevant experiences and training.

In this book's glossary I have defined 'gender flexible pedagogy' as 'gender-sensitive teaching'. This is a simplification, a rather inadequate synonym but perhaps a necessary shorthand for certain uses and contexts. However, if I could simply produce a synonym then I wouldn't have written this book! The term 'gender-sensitive teaching' does not sufficiently implicate the practical, political and theoretical layers that are embedded in a gender flexible pedagogy. **Pedagogy** is a fundamentally relational concept so the term 'gender sensitivity' does not do justice to: relationality; care; versatility; a move away from essentialist ideas about identities and roles.

A gender flexible pedagogy is a way of teaching young children *through* and *about* **gender sensitivity** so that **gender stereotypes** are challenged and gender ceases to straitjacket children's potential. It implies the simultaneous development of gender-sensitive teachers and a gender-sensitive **curriculum** recognising the inter-relatedness of what is taught and how, as well as by whom. A gender flexible pedagogy helps young children themselves to challenge gender stereotypes so that they may grow up to make less gender-constrained choices about their own careers and gender roles in their families and communities.

Why do we need a gender flexible pedagogy?

If society continues to emphasise gender difference, it reinforces the **gender binary** in ways that make it hard for individuals and organisations to cross over, even temporarily. The gender binary creates the limits of what is possible for individual human beings, wider groups of humans and for the much wider society. It is interesting to see that several UK organisations have latched onto the idea of 'limits' in recent times as a way of describing the damage that is done when we emphasise the boundary around men as distinct from women, and masculinities as distinct from femininities. For example, the UK organisation 'Lifting Limits' has chosen this name whilst the Fawcett Society have entitled their recent report 'Unlimited Potential' to underline the possibilities and benefits that will accrue to our young people if we can begin to dismantle gender stereotypes. They tell us that the limitations caused by gender stereotypes 'start early, hold many children back, and cause significant problems across society in later life' (p. 6).

A gender flexible pedagogy is needed to counteract the amazingly strong and persistent stereotyping that exists in the wider society, for example through the way that commercial companies use gender stereotypes to sell their products to children and parents. Indeed, the pervasiveness of gender-stereotypes can be described as the 'wallpaper' of young children's lives (Fawcett, 2020, p. 13).

I have used the metaphor of gender-sensitive antennae throughout this book to describe the need for children and adults to develop an alertness to gender stereotypes. A gender flexible pedagogy in early childhood education (ECE) can make a key contribution to this enterprise. If young children, helped by gender-sensitive teachers collaborating with gender-sensitive parents, can develop gender-sensitive antennae at a young age, they will be able to suss out potential gender limitations which will not then pass into the realms of their unconsciousness and become deeply buried assumptions about societal gender norms.

Why a focus on the early years of education?

In this book, I am promoting the importance of delivering a gender flexible pedagogy for young children but it goes without saying that our gender-sensitive antennae must continue to be sharpened throughout the education system and of course, indeed, throughout our lives. So, why a focus on the early years of education?

It is in the early years of life that we begin to understand our place in the world: the immediate world of family, the wider world of the early education setting and eventually our much wider society. Children are just on the cusp of becoming trapped into gender stereotypes but yet they still have gender playfulness and experimentation because they have not yet, quite, internalised the gender order. Indeed, we have evidence that some of them are quite uncomfortable with gender-conformity prescriptions (Warin & Price, 2020) and may, through their own choices and behaviours, challenge and disrupt the traditional gender order with its limiting and prescribed gender expectations. They may often themselves be leaders in creating an environment where gender stereotypes are challenged. This is one reason why early childhood educators are well positioned to disrupt gender normalising discourses in their pedagogies and practices (Cloughessy & Waniganayake, 2019; Robinson & Diaz, 2006).

The Early Years sector in the United Kingdom and across the globe has always combined elements of education and care. In this book, I have argued that this holistic approach to education should not just be constrained to adult care of children and young people but has the potential to incorporate a dimension of mutual care (Noddings, 2005), children developing kindness towards each other as an integral part of their education, as citizens who care for and about each other.

However, gender stereotypes are implicated in this prescription as we often see that gender roles and stereotypes can stand in the way of the realisation of this vital aim. In particular, we have seen how the traditional association between caring for children and women's work gives a very strong message to boys and girls about the division of care labour in society. Boys and girls need as much opportunity as each other to engage in caring activities and form caring relationships. This is a route to a greater gender equity where boys, girls, men and women share both the burdens and the blessings of care. Potentially the Early Years Education setting could become a beacon of this kind of gender-free 'care-full' citizenship.

The What, Who and How of a Gender Flexible Pedagogy

My intention was to break down the concept of a gender flexible pedagogy into three components to help interested parties, be they practitioners, academics or policy-makers, to think about three questions: the *what*, *who* and *how* of implementing a gender flexible pedagogy. So, I now offer you conclusions to these three main structuring questions.

What

What is a gender flexible pedagogy? We began our investigation of the concept of a gender flexible pedagogy (Chapter 2) by asking about the relevance of curriculum, the content of learning activities. We concluded that gender often features in curricula as part of an 'et cetera' list of foci within broader expressions of values for diversity and equality. Whilst this intersectional approach has advantages, it can sometimes make gender invisible. We are far more likely to develop gender sensitivity, gender-sensitive antennae, if there is something really specific about it on the curriculum for the early years – in guidance documents about what should be taught. I argued that there is an insufficient attention given to gender in the ECE curriculum guidance of most countries although there are some notable exceptions that can provide positive models to emulate. In Chapter 3 we continued to look at the 'what' of a gender flexible pedagogy by investigating some of the many resources that are now available to support stereotype smashing and that can be selected to stimulate and support gender awareness in Early Years education. The resources that I discussed are those that I have become familiar with myself but, doubtless, there are many other such resources available in the United Kingdom and in other countries. I also made an important point about the management of gender-bending resources and activities. Here the content of a gender flexible pedagogy (the available resources and the repertoire of activities) intersects with the skills and imagination of ECE teachers. No amount of brilliant resources can help develop young children's gender awareness and challenge gender stereotyping unless they are used skilfully, creatively and opportunistically by staff who have a will to tackle gender stereotyping. With young children, there is a need to respond spontaneously 'in the moment', so I argued that good resources need to be readily at hand to support the spontaneous discussions that arise as part of classroom inter-actions. In this way Early Years education teachers can harness and create teachable moments and build up a trajectory of discussions and related practices. Part of the ECE teacher's skill set is their capacity to develop a relationship with each child so that their developing knowledge of every individual, and the peer group relations within each class, can be managed carefully. Through their relational skills they can target the use of gender-focused resources, discussions and interventions in peer groups so that gendered patterns of peer choices/toy choices do not become entrenched. The combination of well-chosen resources together with motivated gender-focused teaching reinforces the idea of a gender flexible *pedagogy*, an inseparability from what is taught, who teaches and how.

Who

The next section of the book considered the '**who**' of gender flexible pedagogy, opening up a discussion about the teachers who are implicated in delivering it. This was divided into two chapters considering, firstly, the diversity of the ECE work-force, and secondly, its versatility. The focus on teachers necessitated a discussion of meanings of pedagogy since this is so relevant for the holistic approach to children's well-being and learning that characterises the ECE sector. I emphasised the impor-tance of, and value placed on, the human relationships between all the people who inhabit the world of ECE. I concluded that although there is some widespread rhetoric about the diversification of the ECE workforce, there is insufficient policy and research on race and other dimensions of difference that intersect with gender. However, we noted some good pockets of practice which adopt an intersectional approach to developing a workforce to represent a setting's wider community. This practice includes the recruitment and support of male ECE practitioners as the percentage of men in the workforce is still extraordinarily low. Indeed, certainly within the United Kingdom, this lack of gender diversity makes the Early Years sector the least gender diverse of all the caring professions (Warin et al., 2020). In Chapter 5 we pinpointed ideas about the ECE teacher's flexibility and versatility, a crucial element of a gender flexible pedagogy. The chapter investigated ideas about the allocation of ECE tasks to male and female practitioners. It made the important point that ideas about the complementarity of traditional male and female roles will lead to reinforcement of the classic gendered division of ECE roles that we still see enacted within the family. Instead, the chapter promoted the idea of *interchangeable* rather than *complementary* gender roles and noted that gender balance scripts can lead to a re-gendering rather than de-gendering of the Early Years setting. However, the chapter also pointed out that a rhetoric of gender role interchangeability is easy to preach but not so easy to practice and we looked at how gender stereotypes have a way of sneaking into even the most gender-sensitive practices. I concluded that a gender flexible pedagogy can be enabled through the presence of male teachers but only if they and their female colleagues are open to gender flexibility and versatility.

How?

How can a gender flexible pedagogy be put into practice? Chapters 6 and 7 emphasise relationality and gender sensitivity as essential strategies for the implementation of a gender flexible pedagogy. In Chapter 6, I developed ideas about the importance of care as a principle that is integral to a gender flexible pedagogy – an ethic of mutual care and relationality which emphasises how children can learn to care for each other as well as experience high-quality care from ECE professionals. So, it positions care as both a means and end of ECE policy and practice. The chapter also examined how Early Years settings can work with families to challenge gender stereotypes and model an openness to, and acceptance of, different kinds of families. I concluded that boys and girls need equal opportunities to develop as caring citizens. Linking back to the above conclusions about the diversity and versatility of the workforce, children will be more likely to develop an equality of care practices if they witness both male and female adults modelling care. This pedagogic principle of care can be hindered through the performance of traditional gender roles which limit the caring activities and proclivities of men and boys. In Chapter 7, I examined the concept of gender sensitivity as a cornerstone for bringing about a gender flexible pedagogy. The focus here was on how to develop a gender flexible pedagogy that is practiced consistently across a whole setting – a **whole school** approach. This challenging ideal is the only way to prevent some staff undermining others in the achievement of an overall higher level of gender sensitivity amongst staff. The chapter also investigated the types of gender sensitivity training that may support a whole school/setting in delivering a gender flexible pedagogy. I noted the need to see a much stronger presence of gender issues in **ITT** in order to prepare new teachers to champion a value for smashing stereotypes. Gender sensitivity training can be delivered in an ongoing way through staffroom discussion especially when supported by an independent gender-focused intervention (and this chapter provides several examples). This is especially helpful when some practitioners are resistant. This chapter identified **unconscious gender bias**, together with the related idea of **gender blindness**, and recognised that an unwillingness to tackle and transform gender essentialist beliefs can be found in many ECE settings, just as in wider society. A key link person within the ECE setting, perhaps labelled a 'gender champion', or the setting's manager/leader, has a vital function in sustaining the impetus and an ongoing programme will have better results than a one-off. A specific focus on our uses of gendered language can be a particularly effective way of bringing about gender sensitivity. Above all, gender sensitivity training can work very effectively when it is informal and spontaneous as a response to everyday incidents. A harmonious cycle may develop in a setting where staff develop a high level of gender sensitivity which they then bring to all aspects of their practice with the children, collaboration with parents and a shared vision within staff team relationships, with the possibility of creating widening ripples of gender awareness.

Challenging Questions for Further Reflection

I am aware, as I draw this book to a close, that there are several strands of enquiry that have been apparent throughout and have appeared across several chapters. I would like to draw attention to three of these as I believe they are interestingly difficult to answer and merit further reflection.

Rather than focusing on a *gender* flexible pedagogy should we not be adopting a broader intersectional approach to equality, diversity and inclusion?

This is way of asking a question that has popped up in various places in this book. It occurred in relation to making gender an explicit part of the Early Years curriculum, as well as in relation to the diversification of the Early Years education workforce and to the emphasis of a 'whole school' push for gender sensitivity. It is also relevant to thinking about gender specialism within a teacher's overall work. Another way of asking this question, as 'a devil's advocate', is to ask: do we need to pinpoint gender more than, say, race or social class, other dimensions of social difference that are equally worthy of a focus within children's education? In answering this we run into the danger of pitting a focus on one difference dimension against another, suggesting, for example, that it might be more important to focus on gender rather than race. A truly intersectional approach invites us to hold our attention on the bigger picture of enmeshed strands of social differences rather than teasing them apart. Yet, this approach risks making a single focus, such as gender, invisible within the broader intersectional vision. I gave particular attention to this question in Chapter 2 where I argued that intersectional approaches do not pit one category of social inequality against another but recognise their interdependency. However, I expanded this line of argument to suggest that we may often have to emphasise or even over-emphasise the importance of one single axis of social difference in order to compensate for its relative invisibility. Specific individuals, teachers, settings, research centres, institutions and organisations who are willing to 'stick their necks out' about the need to challenge the gender order are necessary as society's gender champions so that everybody can develop greater gender sensitivity and sharpen their gender-sensitive antennae.

How is a gender flexible pedagogy a challenge to heteronormativity?

Some of the challenging questions about gender in early childhood that are sprinkled throughout this book, can almost be answered with the single word 'heteronormativity' or certainly with the claim that we live in a heteronormative society. For example, I have asked why we so often see a gendered division of labour for ECE practitioners such as males allocated to boisterous play and females to intimate forms of care. Another question I have raised is about why it is so very uncomfortable for men and older boys to consider wearing a dress? A related third question concerns the occasional, but influential, parental hostility that ECE practitioners sometimes witness to their stereotype smashing practices.

Let's consider these questions in a down to earth way. First, we witness the gendered division of labour for staff in Early Years education because the practices and behaviours of people in this sector (and other sectors of the education system and society at large) are often influenced by an uncritical deep-seated belief that children need so-called female influences balanced with so-called male influences, reproducing the heterosexual family composition: a mummy and a daddy. There is a pervasive **gender blindness** to the possibility that men, women and others can behave and perform in flexible ways according to the demands of the situation. This blindness rests on an even stronger, and more invisible assumption that we are 'essentially' male or female. These assumptions are not only about gender and sexuality, but they are also about the very nature of identity – the belief that we have an 'essential' self which is bolstered through consistent repeated behaviours. This deep-seated belief does not allow for masculine femininity and feminine masculinity. It does not allow for a much more fluid and flexible experience of the self, in which identity is chameleon-like, adapting to changing social and cultural contexts (Warin, 2010).

Addressing the second fascinating question about dress-wearing, it is evident that the dress represents the 'other' for men and boys. Dress-wearing is perhaps the most extreme manifestation of gender-crossing, disrupting a deep-rooted gender boundary. A fear of homophobic derision maintains this rule of the gender order. Relatedly, and by way of answer to the third question, it seems likely that homophobia is behind the phenomenon of parents, especially fathers, feeling anxious when their sons engage in female-coded play and dress-up activities. To live in a heteronormative society is not only to make assumptions about heterosexuality as a norm but also to fear homosexuality. We live in a heteronormative homophobic world underpinned by essentialist and individualistic beliefs about our identities. A gender flexible pedagogy can support the gradual move away from such damaging beliefs.

Is the idea of a gender flexible pedagogy a futile concept when viewed against the bigger picture of gender inequalities?

As an optimist, I would argue with the defeatism implicit in this question but I also point out the need to see a gender flexible pedagogy as part of 'joined up' gender thinking. For example, Norway's sequence of gender action plans (Warin, 2018) incorporates gender in early childhood as just one element of a multi-faceted push for gender equality. The planning also includes related gender policies such as parental leave, the gender pay gap and the prevention of violence towards women.

This approach is best summed up by the term 'gender mainstreaming', a term defined by the Council of Europe (2022) as:

> The (re)organisation, improvement, development and evaluation of policy processes, so that a gender equality perspective is incorporated in all policies at all levels and at all stages, by the actors normally involved in policy-making.

Another recommendation for 'joined up gender thinking' comes from the 'Unlimited Potential' report (Fawcett, 2020, p. 6):

> no one part of society can make the change needed when it comes to gender stereotypes – we all have to pull together. Unless we all do so, each of us will fear that changes they make in one area will be overridden elsewhere. But every one of us can make a meaningful change in our own way.

Final Word

The young child is inundated with the gender stereotypes that exist in child-focused marketing and in so much of children's culture. Building up the child's capacity to recognise and question gender stereotypes needs constant reinforcement to counter these straitjacketing influences. Yet, I firmly believe that the continuation of gender stereotyping and the persistence of our gender differentiated, heteronormative world can be disrupted by children and adults who want change. The idea of a gender flexible pedagogy is transformational with the potential to be pioneered in Early Years education and cascaded to other educational contexts and wider society. The concept of a gender flexible pedagogy supports the move away from essentialism and into a dismantling of the gender binary. In this sense, it is a form of post-structuralism in action, based on theories about the rejection of essentialism and fixity and instead valuing an openness to mobility, and possibility.

You may have been reading this book as an ECE teacher or manager, as a student training to teach young children or perhaps as an academic, researcher or policy-maker, or maybe as a parent. In whatever capacity I hope the concept of a gender flexible pedagogy is useful and more importantly useable. A gender flexible pedagogy delivered in Early Years education has the potential to be a vital catalyst for breaking down the damaging constraints of gender norms, stereotypes and heteronormative assumptions. The theory relies on recognising the inseparability of what is taught, who teaches and how with regard to gender. The implementation of a gender flexible pedagogy relies on a state of mind, developed through exposure to gender sensitivity training, supported by well-selected resources and boosted through collaboration with like-minded teachers. Ultimately, it relies on the will of those who are raising the next generation. I hope the theory will motivate you, as Early Years educators, to halt gender essentialism in its tracks. I hope it will arm you to liberate the next generation from the pernicious power of the gender binary so that society can move towards ways of thinking about and experiencing gender that are fluid and flexible.

Glossary

Acorns Research Study An ethnographic study undertaken by Jo Warin and Chris Marlow, in 2017, funded by Childbase Partnership. Acorns (pseudonym) was an unusual setting as it had five male staff at the time of the study. The research aimed to explore how and why male practitioners were being recruited and supported. The research is presented in the book *Men in Early Childhood Education and Care: Gender Balance and Flexibility* by Jo Warin (2018). Findings from this research are referred to throughout this book.

Children's Centres These are organisations for young children together with their families aiming to provide both education for children together with support for their wider families. Many of these were developed under the New Labour government in England and Wales in the late 1990s and early years of the millennium, emerging out of the Sure Start initiative (see below) with a large input of government funding. Many have since been closed or reduced to provision of child-focused early education. Some have survived under local authority control.

CPD This is a commonly used acronym in England and stands for 'Continuing Professional Development', in-service training.

Curriculum 'Plan for learning' (see definition section in Chapter 2). It signifies the menu on offer for children; the content of the work that is planned for children's learning and development. NC is the commonly used acronym for the National Curriculum.

DCSF Department for Children, Schools, and Families in the UK government. This was a short-lived department from 2007 to 2010 when it returned to its former name of Department for Education.

DfE Department for Education, in the UK government.

ECE Early Childhood Education.

ECEC Early Childhood Education and Care.

EECERA European Early Childhood Education Research Association.

EYE Early Years Education.

EYFS Early Years Foundation Stage. This is the statutory framework prescribed by the UK government for children from birth to five years old.

Fatherhood Institute The FI is a small UK charity originally government funded and now funded through a variety of sources. It exists to promote 'involved fatherhood'. It incorporates the organisation MITEY – Men in the Early Years (see below). The FI were key partners in the GenderEYE project.

Fawcett Society A leading UK charity working to challenge gender inequalities in all forms. In recent times this has included a focus on challenging young children's gender stereotypes. In 2020 they produced an excellent report, referred to several times in this book: 'Unlimited Potential. The final report of the commission on gender stereotypes in early childhood'.

Feminist Post-Structuralism The starting point for feminist post-structuralism is the recognition that gender is socially constructed. It challenges the deeply ingrained idea that gender is 'hard wired' or based on innate biological differences between men and women. It is derived from post-structuralist linguistics which breaks down binary thinking. Feminist post-structuralism moves us away from the binaries between men/women, masculinity/femininity recognising that we make up these bounded and fixed categories. It emphasises the shifts and fluidities of identities. It is an invaluable approach for this book that recognises, affirms and promotes 'gender flexibility' (see Chapter 1). Further definitions can be found in MacNaughton (2000), Warin (2018) and Josepehidou and Bolshaw (2020).

Gender Action This is a UK organisation that that aims to promote gender equity in educational settings. In particular it has developed an award scheme for recognising settings that are aiming to develop whole school approaches to challenging gender stereotypes.

Gender Balance This is an approach to the social division of labour that is based on a complementarity of gender roles. It has been used to justify the inclusion of male practitioners in the early years of education on the basis that men and women complement each other. However this thinking denotes an underlying 'gender essentialist' assumption about the fixity of gender differences.

Gender Binary The way we have, traditionally, thought about and created a language about two distinct and opposite forms of gender – masculine and feminine – which are based on and which emphasise biological differences between men and women. This thinking is undergoing a radical upheaval at the present time.

Gender Blindness An inability to see that the ways we experience and talk about gender are socially constructed and therefore open to change. It is a disregard for the importance of gender as a mediating influence in social interactions and fails to take account of the cultural and political influences on gender, assuming that gender differences are innate and fixed. Gender blindness will not help us transform the gender order.

Gender Essentialism Implies the belief that a person's gender is 'hard wired', essential in that it is part of their essence. Linked to biological differences between males and females.

GenderEYE Project This is the name given to a research study, funded by the ESRC from 2018 to 2020 undertaken by researchers at Lancaster University (Jo Warin, Joann Wilkinson and Helen Greaves) together with Queen Maud's University in Trondheim Norway (Kari Emilsen) and the Fatherhood Institute (Jeremy Davies). It aimed to examine both how and why men are recruited into Early Years employment. The findings are central to this book.

Gender Flexible Pedagogy The subject of this book! So, it is difficult to give a quick definition. However, a handy synonym is 'gender-sensitive teaching' with implications for what is taught and how.

Gender Fluidity An emphasis on the changing nature of gender recognising that gender is not fixed but ever changing in fluid ways according to social, cultural and political contexts, changing across time and place. It is closely related to the idea of gender flexibility, the choice of noun depending on the user's preference for bendability or flow.

Gender Sensitivity A key concept in this book. It implies an awareness of how gender is experienced and performed in self and others. It applies to teachers who need this quality in order to recognise and challenge gender stereotypes, and it applies to the ways that children can also be helped to become attuned to sexism and gender stereotypes.

Gender Stereotypes Gender stereotypes are roles or sets of behaviours which simplify and prescribe expectations about what a person can do or become. To a certain extent, stereotypes are inevitable because they create a shorthand, a generalisation about human behaviours in ourselves and in those around us. However, gender stereotypes are harmful because they impose limits on human behaviours, blocking potential growth and barring pathways of possibilities.

GST An acronym used by Josephidou and Bolshaw (2020) for the important principle of Gender Sensitivity Training. This form of training during ITT and CPD enables early childhood education practitioners to question their own gendered assumptions. Gender-sensitive training requires practitioners to be reflexive and self-critical and to surface their own buried unconscious biases about gender (see 'unconscious gender bias' below). It supports them to become much more conscious of how gender stereotypes and assumptions have a limiting impact on all kinds of possibilities for children's learning, growth and development.

Heteronormativity This is quite simply the assumption that heterosexuality is the normal expression of sexuality. It takes the gender binary for granted as it is based on a distinction between two, and only two, opposite gender groups and that sexual relations are only appropriate and 'normal' between people of the opposite sex. Consequently, it is linked to homophobia.

INSET This acronym stands for 'In-service education and training', part of a teacher's continuous professional development. This often takes the form of day or part of day set aside for teachers to attend training sessions to develop their craft or for various kinds of experts to the visit the school or setting.

Intersectionality Crenshaw (2017) and others have recognised the limitations of homogenous, tightly bounded, identity categories such as gender, race or class. Instead their analyses of sociological relations rely on the complexities of inter-woven and interdependent social categories. The concept is nicely summed up by Valocchi (2005) as the 'the crosscutting identifications of individuals along several axes of social difference' (p. 754).

ITT Initial Teacher Training. This refers to the pre-service training for teachers as opposed to in-service CPD, continuous professional development. These terms are currently in use in the UK.

Let Toys Be Toys: Let Books Be Books: Let Clothes Be Clothes These linked organisations commenced with a UK group called Let Toys Be Toys, formed in 2012 in the run-up to Christmas when a group of parents challenged the use of gender stereotypes to sell toys, initially focused on boy/girl distinctions in toyshops. The associated groups, Let Books Be Books and Let Clothes Be Clothes, focused on these closely related aspects of the commercial exploitation of gender stereotypes for marketing to children and their parents. (See relevant references in several places in this book and websites listed in References section).

Lifting Limits This UK organisation exists to 'provide schools with everything they need to challenge gender stereotypes' offering whole school training to 'recognise and correct gender bias' (see website in References list).

MITEY Men in the Early Years. This organisation is embedded in the Fatherhood Institute (see above) and has existed for several years to advocate for more male practitioners to enter into and remain in early childhood education. It has created a MITEY charter for Early Years settings to display and to promote, as a tool for demonstrating an openness to the employment of men. From 2016 to 2020, there was a series of MITEY national conferences aimed at discussing how more men could be brought into the work to gender diversify the profession.

NEU National Education Union in the UK. A large union for teachers of all sorts: including school teachers, lecturers, support staff and school leaders.

Pedagogy This concept is a central one in the book and its meaning is discussed in Chapter 1 and again in Chapter 4. It is more than just a synonym for teaching. It implies the *art* of teaching and incorporates a relational approach to education that emphasises teaching and learning relationships rather than teaching content or teaching skills.

Queer Theory Queer theory emerged as a field of study in the 1990s derived from gender and women's studies. It challenges heteronormative thinking that takes heterosexuality for granted. It is strongly associated with post-structuralist thought because it disrupts traditional, 'essentialist' boundaries and binaries relating to gender and sexuality.

Stonewall Stonewall is a longstanding UK organisation that 'fights for the freedom, equity and potential of LGBTQ+ people everywhere' (see website listed in References list for this book).

Sure Start Based on the longstanding Head Start programme in the United States, Sure Start was the brain child of the New Labour government in the late 1990s, and was well resourced from the government's treasury. It aimed to provide children with a strong start in their early childhood based on ideas about the criticality of the first three years for the well-being of individuals in later life and consequently for society as a whole. The initiative passed into the hands of local government and morphed into the provision of Children's Centres (see above) which then received severe cuts when the government subsequently changed.

Swedish study (Swedish Research Network in Teachers, Gender, and Care) An international network of colleagues, 2011–2014, concerned with gender, teaching and care which began through a Swedish Research Council funded network comprised of Vina Adriany, Eva Gannerud, Annette Hellman, Jo Warin and Inga Wernersson. The network funded Jo Warin's research on male Swedish pre-school teachers, referred to in this book.

Troops to Teachers The Troops to Teachers initiative was launched in the United Kingdom in 2013, emulating a US initiative to enable ex-armed forces personnel to become teachers. It met with much criticism and very little take-up. It closed in 2021.

Unconscious Gender Bias Habituated and subconscious patterns of thought that are based on traditional unquestioned gender norms. Even those people who try to be highly conscious of gendered assumptions can be caught out by their ingrained beliefs about gender. This often shows up in language practices.

Whole School Staff working in chorus on a goal or topic. A tough ideal but one which is much spoken of.

References

Abad, C., & Pruden, S. (2013). Do storybooks really break children's gender stereo-types? *Frontiers in Psychology*, 24. https://www.researchgate.net/publication/269734902_Do_Storybooks_Really_Break_Children's_Gender_Stereotypes

Adriany, V., & Warin, J. (2014). Preschool teachers' approaches to gender differences within a child-centered pedagogy: Findings from an Indonesian kindergarten. *International Journal of Early Years Education*, 22(3), 315–328.

Aistear: The Curriculum Framework for Early Childhood (Ireland). https://ncca.ie/en/early-childhood/

Alexander, R. (2004). Still no pedagogy? Pragmatism and compliance in primary education. *Cambridge Journal of Education*, 34(1), 7–33.

Alexander, R. J. (Ed.). (2010). Children, their world, their education. Final report and recommendations of the Cambridge primary review. Abingdon: Routledge.

Anti-Bullying Alliance. https://anti-bullyingalliance.org.uk/tools-information/all-about-bullying/whole-school-and-setting-approach/what-whole-school-or-setting?

Artino, A. (2007). *Bandura, ross and ross: 'Observational learning and the bobo doll'*. University of Connecticut. https://files.eric.ed.gov/fulltext/ED499095.pdf

Ball, S. (2003). The teachers' soul and the terrors of performativity. *Journal of Education Policy*, 18(2), 215–228.

Ball, S. (2008). *The education debate*. Bristol: Policy Press.

Bandura, A., Ross, D., & Ross, S. A. (1961). Transmission of aggression through imitation of aggressive models. *The Journal of Abnormal and Social Psychology*, 63(3), 575–582. https://doi.org/10.1037/h0045925

Bartholmaeus, C. (2015). Girls can like boy toys': Junior primary school children's understandings of feminist picture books. *Gender and Education*, 28(7), 935–950.

BBC2 Documentary. No more boys and girls: Can our kids go gender free? 16th August, 2017.

Bennet, N., Wood, L., & Rogers, S. (1997). *Teaching through play*. Buckingham: Open University Press.

Bhana, D., Xu, Y., & Emilsen, K. (2021). Masculinity, sexuality and resistance. In D. Brody, et al. (Eds.), *Exploring career trajectories of men in the early childhood education and care workforce*. Abingdon: Oxford, Routledge.

Biesta, G. (2014). Measuring what we value or valuing what we measure? Globaliza-
tion, accountability and the question of educational purpose. *Pensamiento Educa-
tivo. Revista de Investigación Educacional Latinoamericana*, 51(1), 46–57.

Blaise, M. (2005). A feminist poststructuralist study of children 'doing' gender in an
urban kindergarten classroom. *Early Childhood Research Quarterly*, 20(1), 85–108.

Blanco-Bayo, A. (2022). *'CARIÑO IS THE PEDAGOGY.' Assessing 4-year-olds whilst
making sense of their behaviours. An explanatory analysis of policy and practice*. PhD
thesis. Lancaster University.

Bonetti, S. (2018). *The early years workforce: A fragmented picture*. Education Policy
institute. file:///C:/Users/jo/Documents/jos/Lancaster%20uni/Book%20on%20Gender
%20in%20Early%20Childhood%20Education/Chapter%204%20Diverse%20work-
force/Bonetti%20EPI_-Early-Years-Workforce.pdf

Bornstein, M. H., & Arteberry, M. E. (2010). The development of object categorization
in young children: Hierarchical inclusiveness, age, perceptual attribute, and group
versus individual analyses. *Developmental Psychology*, 4(2), 350–365.

Bradbury, A., & Roberts-Holmes, G. (2017). Creating an ofsted story: The role of early
years assessment data in schools' narratives of progress. *British Journal of Sociology of
Education*, 38(7), 943–955.

Bragg, S., Renold, E., Ringrose, J., & Jackson, C. (2018). More than boy, girl, male,
female': Exploring young people's views on gender diversity within and beyond
school contexts. *Sex Education, Sexuality, Society and Learning*, 18(4), 420–434.

British Science Week. https://www.britishscienceweek.org/

Broadhead, P., & Meleady, C. (2008). *Children, families, and communities. Creating and
sustaining integrated services*. Maidenhead: Open University Press.

Brody, D., Emilsen, K., Rohrmann, T., & Warin, J. (2021). *Exploring career trajectories of
men in the early childhood education and care workforce*. London: Routledge.

Browne, N. (2004). *Gender equity in the early years*. Berkshire: Open University Press.

Brownhill, S., Warwick, P., Warwick, J., & Hajdukova, E. (2021). Role model or
'facilitator'? Exploring male teachers' and male trainees' perceptions of the term
'role model' in England. *Gender and Education*, 33(6), 645–660.

Burn, E., & Pratt-Adams, S. (2015). *Men teaching children 3-11*. London: Bloomsbury.

Butler, J. (1990). *Gender trouble. Feminism and the subversion of identity*. London and
New York, NY: Routledge.

Butler, J. (1999). In *Gender trouble. Feminism and the subversion of identity* (2nd ed.).
New York, NY: Routledge.

Chandler, T. (1998). Men as workers in services for young children: Issues of a mixed
gender workforce. In C. Owen, C. Cameron & P. Moss (Eds.), *Men as workers in services for children: Issues of a mixed gender workforce*. London: Institute of Education.

Cho, S., Crenshaw, K. W., & McCall, L. (2013). Toward a field of intersectionality
studies: Theory, applications, and praxis. *Signs: Journal of Women in Culture and
Society*, 38. The University of Chicago Press. http://www.jstor.com/stable/10.1086/
66960

Cloughessy, K., & Waniganayake, M. (2014). Early childhood educators working with
children who have lesbian, gay, bisexual and transgender parents: What does the
literature tell us? *Early Child Development and Care*, 184(8), 1267–1280.

Cloughessy, K., & Waniganayake, M. (2019). Lesbian parents' perceptions of children's picture books featuring same-sex parented families. *Early Years. An International Research Journal*, 39(2), 118–131.

Colwell, J. (2015). *Reflective teaching in early education*. London: Bloomsbury.

Connell, R. W. (1987). *Gender and power*. Oxford: Polity Press.

Connell, R. W. (1997). The big picture: Masculinities in recent world history. In A. H. Halsey, H. Lauder, P. Brown & A. Stuart Wells (Eds.), *Education: Culture, economy and society*. Oxford: Oxford University Press.

Council of Europe Portal. (2022). *What is gender mainstreaming?* https://www.coe.int/en/web/genderequality/gender-mainstreaming#:~:text=Gender%20mainstreaming%20is%20an%20approach,aimed%20at%20designing%20better%20policies

Crenshaw, K. W. (2017). *Intersectionality: Essential writings*. New York, NY: The New Press.

Cushman, P. (2008). So what exactly do you want? What principals mean when they say 'male role model'. *Gender and Education*, 20(2), 123–136.

Davies, B. (2003). In *Frogs and snails and feminist tales; preschool children and gender* (Rev. ed.). Cresskill, NJ: Hampton Press.

Davies, J., Wilkinson, J., & Warin, J. (2020). *GenderEYE toolkit*. https://gendereye.org/outputs/training/

Day, J. (2020). Expert view: Let toys be toys. In L. Rycroft-Smith & G. Andre (Eds.), *The equal classroom: Life changing thinking about gender*. London: Routledge.

Department of Basic Education, Republic of South Africa Curriculum and Assessment Policy Statement. *Grades R – 12. Life skills*. https://www.education.gov.za/Curriculum/NationalCurriculumStatementsGradesR-12.aspx

Department for Children, Schools and Families (DCSF). (2009). *Gender issues in school-what works to improve achievement for boys and girls*. https://dera.ioe.ac.uk/9094/1/00601-2009BKT-EN.pdf

Department for Education (DfE). (2017a). *Supporting mental health in schools and colleges*. https://www.gov.uk/government/publications/supporting-mental-health-in-schools-and-colleges

Department for Education, (DfE). (2017b). *Policy paper: The early years workforce strategy*. REF: DFE 00077- 2017, England. https://www.gov.uk/government/publications/early-years-workforce-strategy

Department for Education (DfE). (2021a). *Teachers' standards guidance for school leaders, school staff and governing bodies*. https://assets.publishing.service.gov.uk/government/uploads/system/uploads/attachment_data/file/1007716/Teachers__Standards_2021_update.pdf

Department for Education (DfE). (2021b). *Statutory framework for the early years foundation stage*. https://www.gov.uk.Early.Years

Department for Education (DfE). (2018). *Gender diversity task and finish group 'improving gender balance and increasing diversity in England's early years education (EYE) workforce' (2018)*. Chaired by David Wright and Jeremy Davies. https://miteyuk.org/

Drag Queen Story Hour. dragqueenstoryhour.co.uk

Drudy, S. (2008). Gender balance/gender bias: The teaching profession and the impact of feminisation, *Gender and Education*, 20(4), 309–323.

Edfelt, D., & Johansson, B. (2012). *Tisdagspiraterna (tuesday – pirates)*. Stockholm: B. Walstrom.

Eidevald, C., Ljunggren, B., & Thordardottir, T. (2021). Professionalisation and gender balance. In D. Brody, K. Emilsen, T. Rohrmann & J. Warin (Eds.), *Exploring career trajectories of men in the early childhood education and care workforce*. London: Routledge.

Eisenstadt, N. (2011). *Providing a sure start. How government discovered early childhood*. Bristol: Policy Press.

Emilsen, K., & Koch, B. (2010). Men and women in outdoor play – changing the concepts of caring from research projects. *European Early Childhood Education Research Journal*, 18(4), 543–553.

Evaristo, B. (2021). *Girl, woman, other*. London: Hamish Hamilton.

Fawcett. (2020). *Unlimited potential. The final report of the commission on gender stereotypes in early childhood*. https://www.fawcettsociety.org.uk/unlimited-potential-the-final-report-of-the-commission-on-gender-stereotypes-in-early-childhood

Fawcett Society. https://www.fawcettsociety.org.uk/

Fielding, M., & Moss, P. (2011). *Radical education and the common school*. London and New York, NY: Routledge.

Fine, C. (2017). *Testosterone rex. Unmaking the myths of our gendered minds*. London and New York, NY: Icon.

Fisher, B., & Tronto, J. C. (1990). Toward a feminist theory of care. In E. Abel & M. Nelson (Eds.), *Circles of care: Work and identity in women's lives* (pp. 35–62). Albany, NY: SUNY Press.

Fletcher, R., St George, J., & Freeman, E. (2013). Rough and tumble play quality: Theoretical foundations for a new measure of father-child interaction. *Early Child Development and Care*, 183(6), 746–759.

Francis, B., & Skelton, C. (2001). Men teachers and the construction of heterosexual masculinity in the classroom. *Sex Education*, 1(1), 9–21.

Gender Action. *The gender action schools award*. https://www.google.com/search?q=Gender+Action&oq=Gender+Action&aqs=chrome.69i57j0i512l5j69i60l2.6376j0j7&sourceid=chrome&ie=UTF-8

GenderEYE project. https://gendereye.org/

Gill, T. (2014). The benefits of children's engagement with nature: A systematic literature review. *Children, Youth and Environments*, 2(24), 10–34.

Gillies, V., Edwards, R., & Horsley, N. (2017). *Challenging the politics of early intervention: who's saving children and why?* Bristol: Policy Press.

Goldberg, J. M., Sklad, M., Elfrink, T. R., Schreurs, K. M. G., Bohlmeijer, E. T., & Clarke, A. M. (2019). Effectiveness of interventions adopting a whole school approach to enhancing social and emotional development: A meta-analysis. *European Journal of Psychology of Education*, 34, 755–782.

Goldstein, H., Moss, G., Sammons, P., Sinnott, G., & Stobart, G. (2018). *A baseline without basis: The validity and utility of the proposed reception baseline assessment in England*. London: British Educational Research Association. https://www.bera.ac.uk/researchers-resources/ publications/a-baseline-without-basis

Golombok, S., Tasker, F., & Murray, C. (1997). Children raised in fatherless families from infancy: Family relationships and the socio-emotional development of children of lesbian and single heterosexual mothers. *Journal of Child Psychology and Psychiatry*, 38(7), 783–792.

Halberstam, J. (1998). *Female masculinity*. Durham, NC: Duke University Press.

Hashmi, S., Vanderwert, R. E., Price, H. A., & Gerson, S. A. (2020). Exploring the benefits of doll play through neuroscience. *Frontiers in Human Neuroscience. Cognitive Neuroscience*, 14. https://doi.org/10.3389/fnhum.2020.560176

Hayward, G., Hodgson, A., Johnson, J., Oancea, A., Pring, R., Spours, K., Wilde, S., & Wright, S. (2005). *The Nuffield review of 14–19 education and training: Annual report, 2004–2005*. Oxford: Oxford University Press.

Haywood, C., & Mac An Ghaill, M. (1996). Schooling masculinities. In: M. Mac an Ghaill (Ed.), *Understanding masculinities*. Buckingham: Open University Press.

Hedlin, M., & Åberg, M. (2019). Principle or dialogue: Preschool directors speak about how they handle parents' suspicions towards men. *Power and Education,* 11(1), 85–95.

Hill Collins, P., & Bilge, S. (2020). *Intersectionality*. Medfort: Polity Press.

Hogan, V. (2012). Locating my teaching of gender in early childhood education teacher education within the wider discourse of feminist pedagogy and post-structuralist theory. Paper presented at the joint AARE/APERA, Sydney. http://files.eric.ed.gov/fulltext/ED542504.pdf

HollySiz – The Light (Clip official) 24th Sept 2014 Youtube. Cecile Cassel. Released in 2013 as video for the album 'My Name is…'. https://www.google.com/search?q=hollysiz+-+the+light+(clip+officiel)&oq=HollySiz-The+light+%5B&aqs=chrome.1.69i57j0i22i30l6.25119j0j15&sourceid=chrome&ie=UTF-8

Hutchings, M., Carrington, B., Francis, B., Skelton, C., Read, B., & Hall, I. (2008). Nice and kind, smart and funny: What children like and want to emulate in their teachers. *Oxford Review of Education*, 34(2), 135–157.

Iceland the act on equal status and equal rights of women and men, No. 10/2008. https://www.ilo.org/dyn/travail/docs/1556/Act-on-equal-status-and-equal-rights-of-women-and-men_no-10-2008.pdf

Icelandic national curriculum guide for preschools ministry of education, science and culture 2011. (2022). (English version). https://www.stjornarradid.is/media/menntamalaraduneyti-media/media/ritogskyrslur/adskr_leiksk_ens_2012.pdf

Institute of Physics (IOP) IOP Campaign. Limit less. Manifesto. Support young people to change the world. Campaign.iop.org.

Institute of Physics (IOP). Limit Less. Teaching without limits. An early years and primary school perspective. IOP. https://www.iop.org/sites/default/files/2021-10/Limit-Less-Teaching-without-limits-Early-years-and-primary-schools-UK-Ireland.pdf

Jagose, A. (1996). In *Queer theory an introduction* (Reprint. ed.). New York, NY: New York University Press. ISBN 978-0814742341.

James, A., & Prout, A. (Eds.). (1990). In *Constructing and reconstructing childhood*. Basingstoke: Falmer Press.

Jennett, M. (2018). *Challenging gender stereotypes through primary education: Stereotypes stop you doing stuff*. Report by National Education Union (NEU). https://neu.org.uk/media/2926/view

Jones, A. (2004). Risk anxiety, policy, and the spectre of sexual abuse in early child-hood education. *Discourse: Studies in the Cultural Politics of Education*, 25(3), 321–334.

Jones, O. (2017). Hatred of LGBTQ people still infects society. It's no time to celebrate. 27th July. *The Guardian*. https://www.theguardian.com

Jones, E., & Reynolds, G. (1992). *The play's the thing: Teachers' roles in children's play*. New York, NY: Teachers' College Press.

Josephidou, J. (2018). *Perceptions of ECEC (early childhood education and care) practitioners on how their gender influences their approaches to play*. PhD thesis. Lancaster University.

Josephidou, J., & Bolshaw, P. (2020). *Understanding gender and early childhood. An introduction to the key debates*. Abingdon: Routledge.

Keddie, A. (2016). Children of the market: Performativity, neoliberal responsibilisation and the construction of student identities. *Oxford Review of Education*, 42(1), 108–122.

Kehilly, M. J. (2002). *Sexuality, gender and schooling: Shifting agendas in social learning*. London: Routledge Falmer.

Konde, P. (2017). *Ra(ce)ising questions about school; analyzing social structures in a Swedish high school*. Department of Cultural Anthropology and Ethnology, Uppsala University.

Lahelma, E. (2000). Lack of male teachers: A problem for students or teachers? *Pedagogy, Culture and Society*, 892, 173–186.

Lally, C. (2020). *Child and adolescent mental health during Covid-19 rapid response*. https://post.parliament.uk/child-and-adolescent-mental-health-during-covid-19/

Layard, R., & Dunn, J. (2009). *A good childhood. searching for values in a competitive age*. London: The Children's Society and Penguin Books.

Lenz Taguchi, H. (2005). Getting personal: How early childhood teacher education troubles students' and teacher educators' identities regarding subjectivity and feminism. *Contemporary Issues in Early Childhood*, 6(3).

Let Books Be Books. https://www.lettoysbetoys.org.uk/time-to-let-books-be-books/

Let Clothes Be Clothes. Campaign group. https://www.letclothesbeclothes.co.uk/

Let Toys Be Toys. https://www.lettoysbetoys.org.uk/about/our-story/

Let Toys Be Toys Report. (2015). *Who gets to play? What do toy ads on UK TV tell children about boys' and girls' play?* http://lettoysbetoys.org.uk/wp-content/uploads/2015/12/LetToysBeToys-Advertising-Report-Dec15.pdf

Letterbox Library. https://www.letterboxlibrary.com/

Lifting Limits. https://liftinglimits.org.uk/stereotypes/gender-stereotypes-in-schools/

Löfdahl, A. (2014). Teacher-parent relations and professional strategies – A case study on documentation and talk about documentation in the Swedish preschool. *Australasian Journal of Early Childhood*, 39(3), 103–110.

Löfdahl, A., & Hjalmarsson, M. (2016). Children's interpretive reproduction of gender-conscious didactic agendas in a Swedish pre-school. In S. Brownhill, J. Warin, & I. Wernersson (Eds.), *Men, masculinities and teaching in early childhood education: International perspectives on gender and care* (pp. 36–46). London: Routledge.

Löfgren, H. (2014). Teachers' work with documentation in preschool: Shaping a profession in the performing of professional identities. *Scandinavian Journal of Educational Research*, 59(6), 638–655.

Lynch, K., Baker, J., & Lyons, M. (2009). *Affective equality. Love, care and injustice.* Basingstoke, Hampshire: Palgrave Macmillan.

MacNaughton, G. (1997). Feminist praxis and the gaze in the early childhood education curriculum. *Gender and Education*, 9(3), 317–326.

MacNaughton, G. (2000). *Rethinking gender in early childhood.* St Leonards: Paul Chapman Publishing.

Mahoney, A. R. (1996). Children, families and feminism. Perspectives on teaching. *Early Childhood Education Journal*, 23(4), 191–196.

Mallozi, C., & Campbell Galman, S. (2016). The ballad of the big manly guy. In S. Brownhill, J. Warin & I. Wernersson (Eds.), *Men, masculinities and teaching in early childhood education: International perspectives on gender and care.* London: Routledge.

Malone, K., & Waite, S. (2016). *Student outcomes and natural schooling.* Plymouth: Plymouth University. https://www.plymouth.ac.uk/uploads/production/document/path/6/6811/Student_outcomes_and__natural_schooling_pathways_to_impact_2016.pdf

Martino, W., & Cumming-Potvin, W. (2020). *Investigating transgender and gender expansive education: Policy and practice.* Oxfordshire: Routledge.

Martino, W., & Rezai Rashti, G. (2012). *Gender, race and the politics of role modeling. The influence of male teachers.* New York, NY: Routledge.

McHale, J. (2022). *Gender, care and career trajectories in early childhood education and care in Ireland.* Unpublished PhD thesis. University College London.

McLaughlin, C., & Alexander, E. (2005). *Reframing personal, social and emotional education: relationships, agency and dialogue.* London: National Children's Bureau.

Meland, A. T. (2020). Challenging gender stereotypes through a transformation of a fairy tale. *European Early Childhood Education Research Journal*, 28(6), 911–922.

Men in Childcare. Organisation. http://www.meninchildcare.co.uk/

Mentally Healthy Schools. *Whole-school approach.* https://www.mentallyhealthyschools.org.uk/whole-school-approach/

Monbiot, G. (2017). *How do we get out of this mess?* https://www.theguardian.com/books/2017/sep/09/george-monbiot-how-de-we-get-out-of-this-mess

MontiKids. https://montikids.com/

More than a Score. https://www.morethanascore.org.uk/

Moser, T., & Martinsen, M. T. (2010). The outdoor environment in Norwegian kindergartens as pedagogical space for toddlers' play, learning and development. *European Early Childhood Education Research Journal*, 18(4), 457–471.

Mukherji, P., & Albon, D. (2009). *Research methods in early childhood.* London: SAGE.

National Council for Curriculum and Assessment. (2004). *Towards A Framework for Early Learning.* Dublin: NCCA.

National Geographic magazine. (2017). *Gender revolution.* Special Issue. https://www.nationalgeographic.com/magazine/2017/01/

National Health Service (NHS) Long term plan. (2019). *Children and young people's mental health.* https://www.longtermplan.nhs.uk/areas-of-work/mental-health/children-and-young-peoples-mental-health/

Noddings, N. (1984). *Caring. A feminine approach to ethics and moral education.* Berkeley, CA: University of California Press.

Noddings, N. (2002). *Educating moral people.* Berkeley, CA: University of California Press.

Noddings, N. (2005). In *The challenge to care in schools* (2nd ed.). New York, NY: Teachers College Press.

Nolan, A., & Raban, B. (2015). *Theories into practice: Understanding and rethinking our work with young children.* Teaching Solutions. http://www.earlychildhoodaustralia.org.au/shop/wp-content/uploads/2015/06/SUND606_sample.pdf

Norwegian Directorate for Education and Training. (2021). *Framework plan for kindergartens (English).* https://www.udir.no/globalassets/filer/barnehage/rammeplan/framework-plan-for-kindergartens2-2017.pdf

Nurseryworld. (2018). *Interview: Helen Perkins.* https://www.nurseryworld.co.uk/other/article/interview-helen-perkins

OECD. (2018). *Education at a glance 2018: OECD indicators.* Paris: OECD Publishing. https://doi.org/10.1787/eag-2018-en

Osgood, J. (2010). Reconstructing professionalism in ECEC: The case for the 'critically reflective emotional professional. *Early Years: An International Research Journal, 30*(2), 119–133.

O'Sullivan, J., & Chambers, S. (2012). *Men working in childcare. Does it matter to children? What do they say?* Report from London Early Years Foundation. https://issuu.com/leyf/docs/leyf-research-report-men-wrking-in-chilcare-2012

Parkin, E., & Long, R. (2021). *Support for children and young people's mental health.* House of Commons Library. https://researchbriefings.files.parliament.uk/documents/CBP-7196/CBP-7196.pdf

Peeters, J., Rohrmann, T., & Emilsen, K. (2015). Gender balance in ECEC: Why is there so little progress? *European Early Childhood Research Journal, 23*(3), 302–314.

Plaisir, J., Thodartottir, T., & Xu, Y. (2021). Societal factors impacting male turnover in ECEC. In D. Brody, K. Emilsen, T. Rohrmann & J. Warin (Eds.), *Exploring career trajectories of men in the early childhood education and care workforce.* Abingdon: Oxford, Routledge.

Price, D. (2018). *A practical guide to gender diversity and sexuality in early years.* London: Jessica Kingsley.

Rahilly, E. R. (2015). The gender binary meets the gender-variant child. *Gender and Society, 23*(3).

Rankin, S., & Beemyn, G. (2012). Beyond a binary: The lives of gender-nonconforming youth. *About Campus, 17*(4), 2–10. https://doi.org/10.1002/abc.21086

Renold, E. (2005). *Girls, boys and junior sexualities: Exploring children's gender and sexual relations in the primary school.* London: RoutledgeFalmer.

Rippon, G. (2019). *The gendered brain: The new neuroscience that shatters the myth of the female brain.* London: Bodley Head.

Roberts-Holmes, G., & Bradbury, A. (2017). Primary schools and network governance: A policy analysis of reception baseline assessment. *British Educational Research Journal*, 43(4), 671–682.

Roberts-Holmes, G., & Moss, P. (2021). *Neoliberalism and early childhood education: Markets, imaginaries and governance*. London: Routledge.

Robinson, K. (2013). *Innocence, knowledge and the construction of childhood. The contradictory nature of sexuality and censorship in children's contemporary lives*. New York, NY: Routledge.

Robinson, K. H., & Diaz, C. J. (2006). *Diversity and difference in early childhood*. Open University Press.

Robinson, K., Smith, E., & Davies, C. (2017). Responsibilities, tensions and ways forward: Parents' perspectives on children's sexuality education. *Sex Education*, 17(3), 1–15.

Rohrrman, T., Brody, D., & Plaisir, J. (2021). A diversity of cultural and institutional contexts. In D. Brody, K. Emilsen, T. Rohrmann & J. Warin (Eds.), *Exploring career trajectories of men in the early childhood education and care workforce*. Abingdon: Oxford, Routledge.

Roots of Empathy. https://www.eyalliance.org.uk/roots-empathy-uk

Rose, J. (Ed.). (2009). In *Independent review of the primary curriculum*. London: Department for Children, Schools, and Families.

Rowe, K. E. (2010). Feminism and fairy tales. *Women's Studies an Inter-Disciplinary Journal*, 6(3), 237–257.

Rycroft-Smith, L., & Andre, G. (2020). *The equal classroom: Life changing thinking about gender*. London: Routledge.

Sando, O. J. (2019). The outdoor environment and children's health: A multilevel approach. *International Journal of Play*, 8(1), 39–52.

Sargent, P. (2004). Between a rock and a hard place: Men caught in the gender bind of early childhood education. *The Journal of Men's Studies*, 12(3), 173–192.

Short, R., Case, G., & McKenzie, K. (2018). The long term impact of a whole school approach of restorative practice: The views of secondary school teachers. *Pastoral Care in Education*, 36(4), 1–12.

Shuayb, M., & O'Donnell, S. (2008). *Aims and values in primary education: England and other countries. Interim report*. Cambridge: NFER, University of Cambridge and Esmee Fairburn.

Simon, B. (1981). Why no pedagogy in England? In B. Simon & W. Taylor (Eds.), *Education in the eighties: The central issues* (pp. 124–145). London: Batsford.

Síolta: National Childhood Network. *The national quality framework for early childhood education (Ireland)*. https://www.ncn.ie›information-resources›siolta

Skelton, C. (2001). *Schooling the boys: Masculinities and primary education*. Buckingham: Open University Press.

Skolverket. (2010). *Läroplan för förskolan Lpfö98. Reviderad 2016 (curriculum for the preschool Lpfö98. Revised 2016)*. Stockholm: Skolverket.

Skolverket. (2021). *Curriculum for the pre-school* (translated from Swedish into English). https://www.skolverket.se/getFile?file=4049

Smashing Stereotypes. https://www.britishscienceweek.org/plan-your-activities/smashing-stereotypes/?gclid=EAIaIQobChMI28mH_ee29gIVloFQBh0pPghKEAAYASAAEgKJKfD_BwE

Smith, P. (1986). Exploration, play and social development in boys and girls. In D. Hargreaves & H. Colley (Eds.), *The psychology of sex roles*. London: Harper and Row.

Stonewall. https://www.stonewall.org.uk/schools-colleges

Sumsion, J. (1999). Critical reflections on the experiences of a male early childhood worker. *Gender and Education*, 11(4), 455–468.

Sweet, E. (2015). *TEDxTalk/Elizabeth V. Sweet, PhD*. Elizabethvsweet.com.

Tembo, S. (2020). Black educators in (white) settings: Making racial identity visible in early childhood education and care in England, UK. *Journal of Early Childhood Research*, 19(1), 70–83. https://doi.org/10.1177/1476718X20948927

Thijs, A., & Van Den Akker, J. (2009). *Curriculum in development*. Amersfoort: Netherlands Institute for Curriculum Development, SLO, Enschede.

Thorne, B. (1993). *Gender play: Girls and boys in school*. New Brunswick, NJ: Rutgers University Press.

Thurer, S. L. (2005). *The end of gender*, New York, NY and Abingdon: Routledge.

Tobia, J. (2016). Gender neutral pronouns. How to use them. Everything you ever wanted to know about gender-neutral pronouns. *Time Magazine*. https://time.com/4327915/gender-neutral-pronouns/

Tronto, J. C. (2006). Vicious circles of privatized caring. In M. Hamington & D. Miller (Eds.), *Socializing care: Feminist ethics and public issues*. Lanham MD: Rowman and Littlefield.

UNICEF. (1989). *The United Nations convention on the rights of the child*. Downloads. unicef.org.uk

UNICEF. (2007). *Child poverty in perspective: An overview of child wellbeing in rich countries, Innocenti report card 7*. Florence: Innocenti Research Centre.

United Nations. (2021). *17 Sustainable development goals to transform our world*. https://www.un.org/sustainabledevelopment/

Valocchi, S. (2005). Not yet queer enough: The lessons of queer theory for the sociology of gender and sexuality. *Gender and Society*, 19(6), 750–770.

Vollans, C. (2016). Fluid thinking. *Nurseryworld Magazine*. Mark Allen Group.

Walkerdine, V. (1981). Sex, power and pedagogy. *Screen Education*, 38, 14–24.

Warin, J. (1998). *The role of gender in the young child's construction of self within the social context of early school experiences*. Unpublished PhD thesis. Lancaster: Lancaster University.

Warin, J. (2000). Gender consistency at the start of school. *Sex Roles*, 42(3–4), 209–231.

Warin, J. (2006). Heavy-metal humpty dumpty: Dissonant masculinities within the context of the nursery. *Gender and Education*, 18(5), 523–539.

Warin, J. (2010). Stories of self: Tracking children's identity and wellbeing through the school years. Stoke-on-Trent: Trentham, 1–212.

Warin, J. (2016). Pioneers, professionals, playmates, protectors, 'poofs' and 'paedos': Swedish male pre-school teachers construction of their identities. In S. Brownhill, J. Warin & I. Wernersson (Eds.), *Men, masculinities and teaching in early childhood education: International perspectives on gender and care*. London: Routledge, 165–106.

Warin, J. (2017). Creating a whole school ethos of care. *Emotional and Behavioural Difficulties, 22*(3), 188–199.

Warin, J. (2018). *Men in early childhood education and care: Gender balance and flexibility.* Palgrave Pivot. Cham: Palgrave Macmillan.

Warin, J. (2019). Conceptualising the value of male practitioners in early childhood care and education: Gender balance or gender flexibility. *Gender and Education, 31*(3), 293–308.

Warin, J., & Adriany, V. (2017). Gender flexible pedagogy in early childhood education. *Journal of Gender Studies, 26*(4), 375–386.

Warin, J., & Gannerud, E. (2014). Gender, teaching and care: A comparative conversation. Editorial. Special Issue. *Gender and Education, 26*(3), 193–200.

Warin, J., & Price, D. (2020). Transgender awareness in early years education (EYE): 'we haven't got any of those here'. *Early Years, 40*(1), 140–154.

Warin, J., Wilkinson, J., Davies, J., Greaves, H., & Hibbin, R. (2020). *Gender diversification of the early years workforce; recruiting and supporting male practitioners.* Project Report. https://gendereye.files.wordpress.com/2020/10/gendereye-final-end-of-project-report-28-oct.pdf

Warin, J., Wilkinson, J., & Greaves, H. M. (2021). How many men work in the English early years sector? Why is the low figure so 'stubbornly resistant to change'? *Children and Society, 35*(6), 870–884. Epub ahead of print…

We need diverse books. https://diversebooks.org/

Weare, K. (2004). *Developing the emotionally literate school.* London: SAGE.

Wee, S., Kim, K. J., & Lee, Y. (2017). Cinderella did not speak up': Critical literacy approaches using folk/fairy tales and their parodies in an early childhood classroom. *Early Childhood Development and Care, 189*(11), 1874–1888.

Westland, E. (2006). Cinderella in the classroom. Children's responses to gender roles in fairy-tales. *Gender and Education, 5*(3). Published online 28th July 2006.

Whalley, M. (1997). *Working with parents.* London: Hodder and Stoughton.

Wikipedia. (2022). https://en.wikipedia.org/wiki/Pedagogy

Wilby, P. (2018). *The counterculture class warrior who turned to Gove.* https://www.theguardian.com/education/2018/oct/09/counterculture-class-warrior-turned-to-gove

Wilkinson, J., & Warin, J. (2021). Men-only support spaces in early years education: A step towards a gender diverse or a gender divided workforce? *Gender and Education, 34*(4), 478–493. https://doi.org/10.1080/09540253.2021.1990221

Williams, C. (1995). *Still a man's world: Men who do women's work.* Berkeley: CA: University of California Press.

Wood, E., & Attfield, J. (2013). In *Play, learning and the early childhood curriculum* (3rd ed.). London: SAGE.

Wright, D., & Brownhill, S. (2019). *Men in early years settings. Building a mixed gender workforce.* London: Jessica Kingsley.

Xu, Y. (2020). Does the gender of a practitioner matter in early childhood education and care? Perspectives from Scottish and Chinese young children. *Children and Society, 34*(95), 354–370.

Xu, Y. (2021). Challenging gender stereotypes through gender-sensitive practices in early years education and care. *Early Education Journal*, 93, 1–16. Early Education, The British Association of Early Childhood Education.

Xu, Y., Brooks, C., Gao, J., & Kitto, E. (2020a). *From global to local: How can international 0–3 curriculum frameworks inform the development of 0–3 care and education guidelines in China?* London: UCL Institute of Education, Centre for Teacher and Early Years Education. https://discovery.ucl.ac.uk/id/eprint/10103137/

Xu, Y., Warin, J., & Robb, M. (2020b). *Beyond gender binaries: Pedagogies and practices in early childhood education and care. (ECEC) Early Years An International Journal of Research and Development*, 40(1), 1–4.

You Be You. https://www.youbeyou.co.uk/

Young, M. (1971). *Knowledge and control. New directions for the sociology of education.* London: Collier-Macmillan.

Young, M. (2008). *Bringing knowledge back in. From social constructivism to social realism in the sociology of education.* London: Routledge.

Index